From Germantown to Steinbach

A Mennonite Odyssey

From Germantown to Steinbach

Daniel Hertzler

Herald Press
Scottdale, Pennsylvania
Kitchener, Ontario
1981

Library of Congress Cataloging in Publication Data

Hertzler, Daniel.
    From Germantown to Steinbach.

    1. Mennonites—United States. 2. Mennonites—
Canada. I. Title.
BX8116.H47   289.7'73   80-28913
ISBN 0-8361-1949-5 (pbk.)

Cover photos by David Hiebert. Other photos by Mary
Hertzler, except pages 16, 92, and 201 by Daniel
Hertzler; page 187 by Jan Gleysteen; and page 191 by
David Gleysteen. Scripture quotations are from the
Revised Standard Version of the Bible, copyrighted 1946,
1952, © 1971, 1973.

FROM GERMANTOWN TO STEINBACH
Copyright © 1981 by Herald Press, Scottdale, Pa. 15683
    Published simultaneously in Canada by Herald Press,
    Kitchener, Ont. N2G 4M5
Library of Congress Catalog Card Number: 80-28913
International Standard Book Number: 0-8361-1949-5
Printed in the United States of America
Design by David Hiebert

81 82 83 84 85 86 10 9 8 7 6 5 4 3 2 1

To the representatives
of 31 Mennonite congregations
who told their stories,
confessed their failings,
and shared their hopes.

Contents

Especially for Henry Penner

Dear Henry:

I am addressing this to you because you spoke to me directly at the Bridgeway Community Church in Swift Current, Saskatchewan, the first Sunday after Easter. You put into words a concern about my visit to your church which was doubtless on the minds of others who did not mention it openly. You said, as I recall, something like this: "I hope you won't mention the bad points of our church. Some of these writers are always looking for the bad things."

I acknowledged your concern and promised rather carelessly to follow your suggestion. But your request has stayed with me in spite of my careless response, for it had been on my mind from the beginning of this project. I started out to do a series of congregational profiles based on visits to Mennonite congregations around the perimeter of the United States and Canada. I wanted to present these congregations so that others might get to know them.

I started at Germantown, Pennsylvania, because this is considered by Mennonite historians the first permanent Mennonite congregation in North America. (The words first and permanent must be used carefully as you will see if you read my first chapter.) A specific reason for starting at Germantown is that the 300th anniversary of its founding is due in 1983. Wouldn't it be interesting, I thought, to visit Germantown and to follow this with visits to a selection of younger congregations of various Mennonite groups to see how it is going with them?

So that is what my wife, Mary, and I set out to do. The results appear in the following chapters. Now in response to your request for a good report, let me note the following.

This is a biased report. My bias is in favor of the Mennonite Church. I wanted to make these visits because I work for and with the Mennonite Church, and I am interested in its progress and welfare. On the other hand, I aspire to be a responsible journalist. I wanted the report I have written to be truth, not half-truth.

So here is what I have done. I requested permission from pastors of congregations to make these visits. In most cases I think they cleared this with the church council. I asked to meet a variety of persons: those who know the history, those in positions of responsibility, persons new in the congregation. Sometimes the pastors went with us to see these people. At other times we went alone.

Most of what I have written is based on these interviews. In the main it is positive, but occasionally some of these people indulged in self-criticism for themselves or the congregations. Perhaps someone disagreed with a strategy being followed or direction being taken. Unless they specified that what they said was not for publication, I felt free to use it. On occasion these comments dropped to what seemed to me the gossip level and then I ignored them.

I have tried to let the message grow out of the stories. But being an editor, I couldn't resist editorializing at times. I have not tried to make the reports strictly uniform, but as my interests were always basically the same, many of the same themes are repeated. I wondered whether it would be difficult after writing a dozen of these to find a new slant for a new chapter, but something always emerged.

My wife, Mary, participated in most of the interviews, occasionally helped with the questions, and served as the first reader of each chapter as I wrote it in a motel room somewhere in the United States or Canada. We usually had heard the same things, but at times there were divergences which we needed to resolve. She also took almost all of the photos which appear in the book.

The visits on which these chapters are based were made between June 1979 and April 1980, the majority during a 13,000-mile trip taken between early January and late April 1980. Except for the first chapter, the research was done on location and is based on the interviews, plus occasional documents supplied by congregational leaders. For the Germantown story, in addition to a visit there, we later went to the Mennonite archives in Goshen, Indiana, and examined records bearing on the history of this congregation.

Thirty-one Mennonite congregations are included in this survey. Some of the visits were quite brief and the reports will indicate as much. Other contacts were extended to three or four days.

So there you have it, Henry (and other readers). I have tried to give a true and fair account, to paint a picture of your church about which you can say, "That really looks like us." If it is not really an accurate view, I can only say that it was my intention to write truth, not falsehood.

I am grateful to the congregational representatives who took the time to tell their stories and those who provided hospitality. Such an endeavor was possible only with the cooperation of many. Thanks is due to Mennonite Publishing House for a sabbatical from my work as editor of *Gospel Herald* of which a part was used for the trip. Thanks also to Jean Cavanaugh who translated the author's marvelous handwriting into legible typewritten prose.

Daniel Hertzler
Scottdale, Pennsylvania

From Germantown to Steinbach

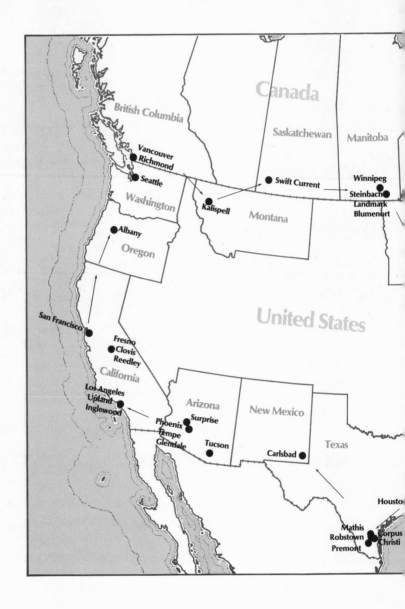

The second Germantown meetinghouse, erected in 1770, renovated and enlarged about 1900, still in use.

1
The Burden and the Promise

There it sits, moldering in the sun, an ancient gray stone building surrounded by the graves of people who used it generations ago. It is the Mennonite meetinghouse at Germantown, Pennsylvania, site of the first permanent Mennonite settlement in North America.

The words *first* and *permanent* are used advisedly. There were Mennonites in the American colonies before 1683, but the one earlier attempt at a Dutch Mennonite settlement at Horekill on the Delaware River was destroyed by the British. And indeed, when one scrutinizes the list of the 13 families who came to Germantown in the fall of 1683, it is found that 12 were Quakers!

But like the source of a river, the history of a people must begin somewhere and Mennonite historians have concluded that Germantown is the place to begin the story. The first drop of water in the North American Mennonite river was Jan Lensen and his family. Jan was a Mennonite weaver from Crefeld in North Germany. With 12 Quaker families, most of whom were former Mennonites and some of whom later reverted to the Mennonite faith, he arrived at

Philadelphia on October 6, 1683. On October 24, Germantown was laid out, six miles from Philadelphia.

Today Germantown is an integral part of Philadelphia. In 1683 the two were separated by six miles of wilderness. Since Germantown was founded only a year after Philadelphia, why was it necessary to go six miles into the woods? There is no clear answer, but one can venture a few surmises. Although Pennsylvania was an open colony, not restricted like Massachusetts, Philadelphia was English and these settlers were German. Evidently the lure of the (somewhat) open spaces already was upon them and in a pattern to be much copied in the next two centuries, they sought their destinies on the "frontier."

The Germantown story is symbolic of the Mennonite experience in America. The Germantown Mennonites were never numerous. The congregation's membership peaked at 99 in 1712. From here it went down and has several times almost died out. Throughout most of its history, Germantown has been marginal to the North American Mennonite experience. Yet it never completely went under and as one views its history, there were occasional key actions which showed that the congregation was more aware of its times than many other Mennonite congregations.

Indeed, is this experience not symbolic of North American Mennonites in our relation to our society? Never large, we have struggled against proselytizers on all sides. We have seen some of our most aggressive and intelligent people leave the church. Such defections have made us unsure of ourselves, and have led us at times to copy the methods of our neighbors instead of using our native means of church building. Yet somehow a tradition has been preserved which, if not the ultimate, is being recognized as authentic. Can it be that both our church as a whole and Germantown as our symbol are coming into a time of greater fruitfulness?

Mary and I went to Germantown on a weekend in early June. It was a pilgrimage taken with an eye to the coming of 1983, and the first contact in a series of congregational visits which ended at Steinbach, Manitoba, nearly a year later.

What we found at Germantown was notable because it was ordinary. One might have been at almost any Mennonite church in North America. Of course there were specific Germantown touches. This was, after all, the oldest Mennonite meetinghouse in North America still in use as a place of worship. The adult Sunday school class led by John L. Freed and meeting in the historical museum rarely meets without visitors present. The Sunday we were there it seemed there were more visitors than regulars. Included was a woman from the local community college who wanted to learn about Mennonites. But the lesson was from an Old Testament text in the Uniform Series and, as often happens in a Mennonite Sunday school, the time ran out before the issues were solved. (I don't remember specifically what the issues were, but doesn't this always happen?)

The worship service with perhaps 75 in attendance also was quite traditional. Did we expect something else? A Mennonite bulletin gave the order of service. Congregational elder Roman Stutzman led the meeting. Farid Wissa, music director, provided flamboyant music leadership. A visiting preacher spoke from 1 Peter 2:4-17 with an eye to the historical reality of Germantown. A potluck meal followed in honor of visitors, as the bulletin stated, so that guests could "meet the congregation and experience our 'urban' hospitality."

According to *Mennonite Yearbook*, Germantown has a membership of 29, with three ministers, Roman Stutzman, John L. Freed, and Gilmer Schmidt. (They told us locally

that Farid Wissa is minister of music.) That is a high ratio of
ministers to members, but none is supported by the congregation, and as Freed remarked, precise membership
statistics are not a high priority for the congregation. A functioning member is one who participates in the faith
experiences and work of the congregation. A certain loose
endedness is in keeping with the congregation's history.

As one views Germantown's past, there are notable peaks
and valleys. This is no doubt true of any congregation, but
because of its small size and precarious position, Germantown's crises, ambiguities, and moments of glory seem
larger than life.

The first crisis involved whether to organize at all. The
early Mennonite community was a small island in a Quaker
sea and might have been absorbed by the Quakers. For the
first few years, they evidently worshiped with them, but by
1690 a visitor from Holland found a group of persons opposed to Quakerism who met each Sunday to hear a "Men-
nist" read from a book of sermons. In that year (or 1698, the
date is not certain) the Mennonites chose William Rittenhouse as preacher and Jan Neuss as deacon.

The second crisis came in 1707-1708 over the integration
of the Palatine Mennonites who kept to themselves for a
year after arrival. By 1708 they agreed to integrate with the
North Germans of the Germantown congregation. This was
a crucial year. The congregation erected the first log church
building and ordained three deacons and two preachers.
There was the first American Mennonite baptismal service
and the first communion. Eleven persons were baptized,
bringing the membership to 45. When one recalls that the
Quakers do not practice literal observance of either of these
ordinances, it appears that 1708 was a breakthrough for
American Mennonites, a determined effort to practice their

own traditional faith. In this they were an exception to the Lutheran and Reformed German colonists whose religious life at this time was in disarray, as described by Julius F. Sachse. In *The German Sectarians of Pennsylvania* he tells of "the forlorn religious condition" of the Germans in Pennsylvania "most of whom, with the exception of the Mennonites, who had kept a corporate organization, had gradually fallen away from the faith of their fathers."

Indeed, it is reported that by 1712 the Germantown membership had more than doubled, to 99. However, this already included the Palatine settlement at Skippack out in the country and from here on Skippack was to increase while Germantown decreased. The movement was toward the country and for the next two centuries American Mennonitism was to be essentially rural. The comparatively urban Germantown congregation barely existed at the edge, unable to hold enough of the children to maintain a viable tradition. By 1770 when the present building went up, the congregation was down to 25 members. In 1839 it nearly died.

In the middle of the century it got caught up in a division of the Skippack Mennonites brought on by an aggressive leader named John Oberholtzer. In 1884, only months after celebrating its 200th anniversary, the pastor resigned and offered to give church letters to all. But a core of persons would not leave. In the early 1900s, a Methodist minister named John W. Bayley became concerned about the state of the building. According to his obituary in *Mennonite Yearbook and Almanac*, 1922, "The congregation was small, the church building in a dilapidated condition, and preaching services rarely held. He at once went about renovating the building.... Later, a new Sunday school building of stone was erected."

Yet in spite of its marginal existence and perilous state, the Germantown congregation has had its moments of glory. It should be recognized for a certain pioneering spirit which has never completely left it. The first of these moments was a protest against slavery in 1688, only five years from the founding of the colony. Now it is appropriate to note that the four persons who signed this protest were not at that time practicing Mennonites, but three are said to have come from the Mennonites, and one of the three later rejoined them. Both Quaker and Mennonite historians believe that Mennonite thinking affected the protest. The protest was addressed by German Quakers to English Quakers and it is not certain that any concrete action came of it. But this was 175 years before the Emancipation Proclamation.

At Germantown also was held the first American Mennonite conference in 1725. This conference adopted the 1632 Dordrecht Mennonite Confession of Faith which was printed within two years for the use of American Mennonites. The congregation has also left some records from the late 19th century which indicate a sense of identity and purpose. (Indeed, how many Mennonite congregations were keeping records in the 19th century?)

According to a document of October 23, 1869, the Germantown congregation had seven standing committees! There was (1) a committee of welcome; (2) a committee of invitation "to kindly invite all they can to visit the church, always guarding against drawing from other churches to fill our own"; (3) a committee of sympathy; (4) a committee for the poor; (5) a committee on Sabbath school; (6) a committee on teaching; and (7) a committee on music. However, committees do not make a church, and the following spring in a report to the district conference, Secretary Samuel Rittenhouse wrote: "State of the church harmonious but not as well attended as is desirable, rather lukewarm." And evidently the decline continued.

The most recent crisis in the Germantown experience came one hundred years later, in the late 1960s. Only a few older people were left. Yet they were old people with some vision. The recent revival at Germantown can be traced to many, but the names of Walter and Eleanor Temple, a brother and sister, keep coming up when you talk about the modern history of Germantown. It appears that they performed two crucial functions. One was to maintain contact with the official Mennonite Church, and the other was to open their arms to younger people who began coming to the church in the early 1970s.

During this period, the congregation's ties to the Mennonite tradition were quite tenuous. Although it was a member of the Eastern District of the General Conference Mennonite Church, there is a story of a congregational dance during World War II as a send-off for young men leaving for military service. Also younger Mennonites coming in the '70s were scandalized by an American flag in the church building.

Yet, as reported by Cornelius Krahn, as early as 1922, C. E. Krehbiel of the General Conference Mennonite Church had stopped in Germantown. Walter Temple and he agreed that the General Conference should become involved "so that the witness of the congregation could continue." Accordingly, the General Conference passed a resolution at Freeman, South Dakota, on September 6, 1922, "that we encourage movement to maintain the Historic Germantown Mennonite Church."

The mills of the church grind slowly. So it was another 25 years, in 1947, before Walter Temple himself could present this case to the Historical Committee of the Church, and another six years before the founding of the Germantown Mennonite Church Corporation which now held the title to keep land pirates from taking over the property and razing the building.

But the congregation was dying. And yet, as before, it would not die, though its vital signs continued feeble. At a corporation meeting in the summer of 1968 Walter Temple pointed out that the first 13 families who came to Germantown were not rural. "We think of Mennonites as rural people," he said, "but the Mennonites were also city people." In the fall of 1970, the old corporation was dissolved and a new broader one organized which included wider Mennonite representation. The new corporation's first decisive action was to invite Melvin and Verna Gingerich to come to Germantown to launch an information center. So entered Mennonite Church historian Melvin Gingerich and his wife, Verna, in the fall of 1971 with a vision to combine history and active church life. About the same time came Wesley Mast and later Rick Mojonnier to work in a ministry to Mennonite students. In addition a number of young Mennonites came—some radical—looking for a church home or an opportunity to serve. In other words, there came an amalgam of influences to shake the five-member Germantown congregation to its core. Now it was the task of Eleanor and Walter and their peers to be flexible enough to let it happen.

Melvin and Verna Gingerich served at Germantown for less than a year, but they set a direction which is still affecting the corporation and congregation. On October 4, 1972, the corporation board accepted a set of four goals presented by Melvin Gingerich. This should be (1) a witness of history; (2) a witness of service; (3) a witness of education; and (4) a witness of evangelism.

Robert Ulle was one of the younger persons who first went to Germantown in 1972. He had been a member of a Mennonite house church which dissolved. Since he was living in Philadelphia and looking for a Mennonite church, he visited Germantown. He did not go back for five months! Then he tried it again and found that things were beginning to change. "When I began attending," says Ulle, "the few young people who did come admitted they came as much for the cookies after church as anything."

One of the first controversies was over the United States flag in the church building. This was finally solved, according to Ulle, by the older people conceding on the basis of its offense to the young. As Eleanor Temple put it, "Paul says, 'If it offends your brother go along with him.' " This put the young people in the role of the "weak" but they accepted this role to get the issue resolved. So corporation chairman, Stanley R. Fretz, could write to Melvin Gingrich on February 10, 1973, that "the annual Germantown congregational meeting voted to remove the flag from the church, look further into dual membership, and encourage student participation in the congregation."

Franconia Conference was contacted about dual membership and first refused to accept Germantown unless the congregation withdrew from the Eastern District of the General Conference. Later this position was reversed and so now this 29-member congregation is affiliated with both the Eastern District of the General Conference of Mennonites and the Franconia Mennonite Conference.

The Gingerichs were succeeded as corporation administrators and directors of the Germantown Information Center by Roman and Marianna Stutzman, a pastoral couple experienced as Voluntary Service directors in Kansas City. In a report of their work on October 1973, the Stutzmans wrote, "We are situated in one of the most unique areas in the city of Philadelphia. Perhaps, also, it is one of the greatest mission fields in the city. We question whether ... we have the capacity or the personnel to make a pronounced impact.... However, we insist that our very presence ... is in itself a very bold testimony. As we pick up the endless number of cans, bottles, and trash, we *speak* to people and we *listen* to them."

In 1975 the Stutzmans resigned as directors of the Germantown Information Center to accept a post as directors of Wyck House, a historic Quaker home about one block from the church which is described in a leaflet as "Philadelphia's oldest house." They continue, however, as participants in the congregation where Roman serves as a member of the pastoral team and Marianna works with the Ladies Aid.

As one tries to understand the Germantown picture, it is important to see that although the corporation and the congregation are tied together, they are not the same. The corporation functions with a particular interest in the historical significance of the area and its buildings. Members of the congregation have more or less interest in these matters. To some the historical baggage at times seems a burden.

In the last five or six years the congregation has been subject to the stress that comes from bringing in a number of young adult intellectual types. Ruth Fireoved, a member since 1971, gives credit to the Gingerichs and the Stutzmans for the current revival. "Verna and Melvin," she recalls "gained respect from both the 'old' and newer members.... The Stutzmans continued with the work begun by the Gingerichs, and the membership expanded."

But Ruth remembers some experiences which she would not wish to repeat. As a small group seeking to be sensitive, caring, and faithful, the congregation for a time used radical

The old and the young at Germantown: Pam Carter in the historic graveyard. For some, the history is a burden, but others are certain that history and present activity belong together.

consensus as a method of making decisions. But this was finally abandoned when it was not possible to satisfy everyone on certain issues and decisions could not be made. More recently they elected as church council chairman Lynn Brubaker, a cool-headed high school teacher. As described by John L. Freed, Lynn "defines an agenda and can keep people with it. Since he is chairman, the congregation is moving."

John Freed observes that there is in the congregation more than one view of the role of the church. Some want a low-key worship experience which provides succor after a week of confronting the world. Others wish the church to be more active in response to the needs of the area. Some would prefer to locate elsewhere without the burden of the Germantown building as a Mennonite shrine. But Virginia Musser predicts that "much of what happens will depend on the tension (healthy, I hope) between congregation and corporation, the stamina of the corporation and the interests of the congregation. If the burdens continue to be carried by a few, and if the struggles are exhausting, then people will continue to 'burn out' and leave."

Not far from the Germantown Mennonite building is the site of the first Church of the Brethren congregation in the New World. The Brethren no longer have a congregation there, but maintain the building as a shrine. They also have hired a full-time community worker. Leonard Gross, executive of the Mennonite Church Historical Committee, hopes the Germantown Mennonite Church will not go this route. "Many of us would be very disillusioned if it were only a building," he said.

Robert Ulle, who no longer attends at Germantown, still has a clear vision for its possibilities. "The crucial question through Germantown's history," he said, "has been the ability of the lay people to function. Formal leadership has always been a problem, so the church has risen or fallen on the basis of lay leadership. Ulle sees no basic conflict between the history as preserved by the corporation and the mission of the congregation. Indeed he has dreams which could transform the whole area through the combined efforts of congregation, corporation, and Mennonite business development which would bring fresh activity to Germantown.

For the first time in more than two centuries, Germantown is in touch with its roots and in dialogue with a wide Mennonite constituency. What remains to be seen is whether it will be able to devise a living congregational tradition with a balance of mobility and stability.

2
The "Come to Jesus" Church

How do you build a Christian congregation where there was none before? You find some people who can be persuaded to follow Jesus and they become the building blocks. Eula Green has been a member of the Diamond Street Mennonite Church in Philadelphia for more than 20 years. She tells how it happened to her.

Eula moved to Philadelphia about 1950. She had been a Baptist at one time, but did not practice the faith in Philadelphia.

"One day I was scrubbing the steps and saw a man knocking on doors. (His name was Irvin Weaver.) He came to me and asked, 'Do you believe in God?'

" 'What do you think I am, an atheist?' "

" 'Do you want to pray?' "

" 'Not out on the sidewalk. Do you want to come in?' "

"So he came in, read from 1 John, and had prayer. At the end he said, 'Do you feel better?'

"I had felt all right before."

"The next day he came back with Pastor Luke Stoltzfus and they got me to promise that I would come to church.

But I did not go and after two weeks I thought I was rid of them. Then came two elderly ladies, Alma Ruth and Emma Rudy, and somehow I couldn't tell them a lie. But I didn't go that Sunday either, and on Monday they were back. So I finally went to church the next Sunday. I soon decided that I wanted to be a member of this church. I can really say this was the first time after I was in my thirties that I was really happy."

Life as a new Mennonite was not easy or simple for Eula. She had to wear special clothing and her family relationships required attention. "I was separated from my husband and had a child. I met a man and wanted to get married, but I was not divorced from my husband. The church objected and I became quite bitter with the church and with Brother Luke and his wife. But we worked it out."

Today Eula is a strong supporter of Diamond Street Church and works as a teacher aide in the Head Start program which meets in the church building. Because Head Start is supported by the United States government, Eula cannot do all she would like with the children.

"May I sing 'Jesus Is the Rock of My Salvation'?" she asked the teacher on one occasion, but this song was disqualified as too sectarian. "Then how about 'If You're Happy, Clap Your Hands'?" This was allowed. Eula is glad to work with Head Start because it is an opportunity to show love to children who need it.

What else do you do to build a church? Most give some attention to the teaching of children. Barbara Allen Baynard joined the church at the age of eight. She too was attracted by Alma Ruth and Emma Rudy. For her and others they held "lot meetings." I did not get it clear what was done in lot meetings, but I imagine there were games, activities, and inevitably some form of Bible study. For Barbara it was enough to make a start and now she is wife of Diamond Street's assistant pastor, Charles Baynard, and teaches at Bethany Day Care Center sponsored by the Diamond Street congregation and directed by her sister, Margaret Allen.

Other signs of the congregation's concern for the young are the Diamond Youth Programs directed by Jimmy Allen.

Eula Green, who came to Jesus through the persistent efforts of Alma Ruth and Emma Rudy. "I can say this was the first time after I was in my thirties that I was really happy."

These programs include a wide variety of after-school and summer activities beginning at age 5 and continuing into the upper teens. Those in the programs are not necessarily the children of church families. In fact, probably most are not.

"Does this program affect the church?" I wondered.

"Not much," Jimmy replied. "But some have come to find out what this church is about. One did join the church, but then he dropped out because he got in with his old buddies and asked to be taken off the membership list."

The programs have gotten the attention of local people. "We don't have to advertise. The kids line up to get in. People really respect the Mennonite Church in this part of the city. They say they're on the move."

Probably the most important factor in building a congregation is for the leaders to grow in understanding of what it takes to build a church. Former pastor Luke Stoltzfus wishes this growth might have been more rapid. Luke and his wife, Miriam, moved their family to Diamond Street in 1951 and stayed 16 years. He remembers that when they arrived there were three members in the congregation.

One was Sister Jenkins, "formerly Baptist, but now a dyed-in-the-wool Mennonite. She seldom criticized the church, but once she was asked what she would like to change. She replied that she could not 'rejoice in the Lord' the way she would like. I urged her to go ahead and say 'Amen.' "

"Oh no," she said.

"I wish we had become aware of the need to make blacks more comfortable in our church," says Luke. "I guess that was one of the things we had to learn from the foreign field. It was difficult for local leadership to emerge as long as the style was restricted. One of the greatest lacks in home missions work has been the failure to develop indigenous leadership."

As evidence, present Diamond Street pastor Freeman Miller reported that there are six pastors in the Philadelphia area who came up through Diamond Street, but the cultural differences kept them from staying in the Mennonite Church. Now things have changed, according to Barbara Baynard. "When I first came into the Mennonite Church, instead of working with you as you were, they had to change you. You became two persons, one at church, and another at home. Now you can be yourself."

Another step in the growth process observed by Luke is the development of "social systems," or family interrelationships. Now there are families at Diamond Street with more than one generation who have intermarried with families in other Mennonite congregations. A further sign of congregational maturing was the sending of the first "missionary." In the summer of 1979 Mattie Cooper left for a Voluntary Service assignment in Upper Volta.

Mark Miller, a Mennonite housing administrator in Philadelphia, commented on the maturation process of the Diamond Street congregation. "My own feeling is they are pretty well along from being a mission to a congregation with their own identity. A significant change in the past five years has freed people to take responsibility."

The taking of responsibility is fostered by Freeman Miller who operates with organizational principles derived from the book *Servant Leadership* by Robert K. Greenleaf. The organizational plan at Diamond Street seeks to avoid hierarchy and to separate the "thinkers" from the "doers."

Basic to the plan is a group called the "trustees" who are the goal setters for the congregation and monitors of four teams: (1) the service team; (2) the property team; (3) the

pastoral team; and (4) the education team. Goals are set an-
nually in line with "felt needs" of the congregation.

Diamond Street is seeking to function as an integrated
church. "Attendance," said Freeman Miller, "tends to be
roughly 50-50 black and white." However, this balance is
not yet clearly reflected in the leadership. Indeed, although
there is a black assistant pastor "many people don't understand that there is a black/white team because there has
been such a history of white dominance."

"My mission is to 'pray out' a young black leader and
train him to be head pastor along with Charles Baynard.
Then I would not leave, but stay here and assist him. I think
that black leadership does not emerge because it is blocked
at the top."

Former pastor and present bishop Luke Stoltzfus supports
Freeman's vision. "With our many faults and failures, we
have continued to survive and to struggle and to serve. I
believe that by the grace of God and the sanctified wisdom
which He gives when sought, there can be growth in the
days ahead."

What about a building? Does a church need a building to
grow? Except for the Amish and "house" churches, most
congregations assume that a building for meetings and
church activity is a necessary part of congregational life.
Since 1942 Diamond Street has functioned in a three-story
plus basement row house at the corner of Diamond and
Gratz. Its identity as a place of worship is proclaimed by a
plaque by the front entrance on Gratz Street, and a large
sign on Diamond Street which says boldly "Come to Jesus."

Luke and Miriam Stoltzfus raised their family here, but
Freeman and Naomi Miller with their three small daughters
live in a separate house. So the complete facilities are available for church and club activities. At the time we visited, a

Head Start program used the 65-person church auditorium.
As described by Freeman, "A part of the benediction at the
end of the service is to take up your chair and walk" so that
the facility may be ready for Head Start the next day. One
way to make equipment do double duty is to use a child's
workbench from Head Start as the congregation's communion table.

A topic of some excitement at the time of our visit was the
possibility of securing a new and improved meetinghouse as
part of a community center. The center project already had
a complex history and there was still a lot of ground to cover.
As described by Naomi Miller, the community center idea
developed from a concern that Diamond Street should relate
more directly to its neighborhood. Though it had a good
reputation, the church standards were viewed as so high that
people could not expect to meet them. Parents saw Diamond Street as a children's church, not something for them
to take seriously.

How could Diamond Street become known as a viable option?

A survey was taken to find out what need was felt in the
area and housing came to the top. "When we began talking
about housing, our phones began ringing," said Freeman
Miller. If the uninitiated wonder about the concern for housing, they need only walk along Diamond Street a few blocks
from the church. On one side the row houses are inhabited;
on the other they are hulks. When you ask why the difference, the answer is "private ownership." Those who own
the houses they live in keep them in good repair.

The concern for housing led to an interest in a community
center and came to rest eventually on an abandoned four-
story building two blocks from the church. Once it was a
telephone headquarters and then it was taken over by the

Masons. No longer in use, it faced the inevitable assaults by vandals. Someone voiced the dream that Diamond Street Church could acquire and renovate the old Masons' building for a community center.

Having been born, the dream of a community center would not die. Bea Macon, a leader in the congregation, kept saying, "That building is ours. I have faith that we are going to get that building." After some years, Freeman became bold enough to ask the Masons for the building, and eventually it was given to the congregation. Then began the task of seeking $500,000 for the renovation.

After careful investigation, Diamond Street's sponsor, the Mission Board of Lancaster Mennonite Conference, made a beginning grant of $50,000. Plans were to go to private foundations for funds under the assumption that money from government would restrict the program as Eula Green found when she wanted to sing about Jesus in Head Start.

We took a tour of the old building and found a solid shell with good possibilities, but a long way to go. The dream was to use this as a facility for congregational worship and teaching. It would also house the youth work and other congregational service programs. In addition, space would be rented to Head Start and to a whole-health center which would be expected to provide a wide range of medical and psychological services for people of the neighborhood.

Some have expressed doubts about whether Diamond Street can carry through this project successfully. Should they really begin? But as Naomi Miller reported, "People say, 'we in the city are used to failing. We don't care if it takes five to ten years. If we can save the building and get one floor completed, we will consider this a success.' "

Several of our interviews stressed that urban people live under pressure. Charles and Barbara Baynard have six

children. In late 1979, the children ranged in age from 17 to
7. "I work full time," said Barbara, "and Charles works full
time. Sometimes I say good-bye to him one morning and
don't see him until the following evening."

As I reviewed my notes on Diamond Street and
Philadelphia, I was impressed by how much of the conversation involved economic issues. "I sometimes think the bottom line for the church in the city is economic," said
Freeman Miller. He noted also that "many have given up
on the inner city. The population is grasping for hope. Our
big purpose is to counteract futility.

"There is a feeling that people here are at the bottom of
the barrel and need to work their way up and out. But there
is a drift now back toward the center and there may still be a
chance for a community church. Loving people to Christ
around their needs is the concept that works in the inner
city."

John L. Freed, executive secretary of the Philadelphia
Mennonite Council, a service to the six Mennonite congregations in the city, spoke along the same lines. He took us
to the Meetinghouse, a Mennonite project in the center of
the city of Philadelphia which developed out of efforts to
witness in the context of the 1976 U.S. Bicentennial
activities. Its emphasis, he said, is to be a "Christian
presence in the marketplace." It is, in fact, a small specialty
shop featuring especially Mennonite Central Committee
"Self Help" products, craft items produced in Third World
countries.

The Meetinghouse was operated by John Heese, a Mennonite from Saskatchewan who had quit a printing business
for a term of Voluntary Service and was working on this
basis. But even so, the shop was not able to cover its costs.
More importantly, "the Meetinghouse suffers from lack of a

people base—a group of people who can anchor it." Freed envisioned perhaps "an intentional community in the area, persons to work there, get acquainted, and develop a ministry to lonely people. Ninety-five percent of them are unchurched."

He went on to observe that "one of the problems with an urban ministry is that we have more dreams that we can carry out. An issue in urban ministry is the economic factor. We have gathered people who are interested in simple lifestyles, who believe it is sinful to make money. But when you want to get going, you need some capital to move around. You don't hear much talk about a simple lifestyle in the black community.

"A problem," he continued, "is that Mennonites in the city tend to be mobile. This has its roots in American society, where for Protestants the city is not a place to put down roots. When Cortez set out to conquer Mexico, he first burned the boats. White people in the city find it difficult to burn their boats. Not many urban churches have it together," he stated further. "Either it is a white church that's dying, or a Pentecostal church that's struggling. Ninety percent of the successful urban churches are black, but they have the least written about them."

Well at least Diamond Street is 50 percent black, and this is a small attempt to write about it. We went to a morning worship service at Diamond Street. It was "Women's Day." Freeman Miller had said that "inner-city culture tends to be event centered, not regular as the farming community with its weekly rhythms." The chief activity, it appeared, in honor of Women's Day was an extended skit by women of the congregation, the theme of which was that scarcely any of them had time to attend a district women's meeting.

The Sunday school which preceded and the preaching

which followed were typical Sunday morning activities, but
with a local twist. Music and singing were notable. The
hymnal was from the Brethren in Christ. (Perhaps their exu-
berant Wesleyan piety fits the black spirit more than *The
Mennonite Hymnal.*) The piano player was a white student
from Temple University, but I assumed the vigorous music
he played was black music. Too bad Sister Jenkins couldn't
hear it.

My notes on the Sunday school lesson included the question, "Is it possible to be a Mennonite and a policeman at
the same time?" As answer, I have a remark by Freeman
Miller suggesting a difference between serving as a policeman and going to war. Another question raised was,
"What do you worry about?"

Answers included "inflation" and "my daughters being
Christian. I am frightened to send my kids out into the
world, but I have to."

"How do you bring your worries to God?"

"I say a little prayer every day."

The sermon by visiting preacher B. Sam Hart was based
on Joshua 1:1-9, and outlined seven steps to success. The
final one he noted was "obedience to God's will." It was an
upbeat sermon. After it was over and the benediction said,
the chairs were folded and the meeting room rearranged to
be ready for Head Start on Monday morning.

We found the Diamond Street integrated congregation on
the threshold of a new phase in its development, looking
ahead to a larger facility, and broader service. But there
were many difficulties. "Maybe it won't work," said
Freeman Miller. "But if you have a group of people so determined, you need to try."

3
Under the Wings of the Navy

As we followed directions to Philip Miller's home in rural Chesapeake, Virginia, two strange looking planes circled low. They did not seem to be crop dusters and we wondered what mission would keep them flying so near the ground.

It was later explained to us that they were radar planes from the nearby airfield for the training of U.S. Navy pilots. Navy planes fly day and night over the Mt. Pleasant Mennonite community. Indeed, although this church stands firmly for the gospel of peace, the rural nature of the Mt. Pleasant area has been preserved in part by the presence of the U.S. Navy. The noise of the Navy pilots' takeoffs and landings has inhibited development of the land for housing. So the dairy farmers have been able to continue raising feed for their cows. And dairyman James Bergey affirmed that the noise does not bother the cows.

It is a strange complementary relationship. While the Mt. Pleasant Mennonites would do all they can to keep their sons from joining the Navy, they would be the first to acknowledge that their relative prosperity is dependent on the extensive Naval installations in the greater Norfolk area. As

Philip Miller, resident bishop and one of three pastors at the Mt. Pleasant congregation. "We have discovered that one pastor can minister to a certain segment, and another to another."

Merlin Miller put it, "Unless the country goes broke, the Navy's going to spend money."

The Mt. Pleasant community is one of two founded by Mennonites in southeast Virginia near the beginning of this century. The other was at Denbigh on the bank of the Warwick River. In both there was a gathering of like-minded Mennonite families from various areas of the United States. Settlers in both purchased worn-out plantation land and set out to build it into a high state of fertility. In each there was also a determined effort to form a colony of heaven.

The two developed at a similar rate for 50 years. Then urbanization began to engulf Denbigh, while the presence of the Navy saved Fentress. Although the rural land is now incorporated into the city of Chesapeake, there were still some Mennonites farming when we visited there early in 1980. But there was also an ongoing contest between the Navy and the city. The city wanted to expand housing. But the residents of the houses complained about the noise of the planes. So the Navy responded by buying a large amount of land. The Navy's purchase encroached upon the farmland and will eventually put some of the farmers out of business.

As explained by Bishop Philip Miller, the land will be available for rental by farmers. But according to the law, each year the Navy must put it up for bids. Thus a dairy farmer could not be sure that a given plot would be available to him on a regular basis, and so could not count on being able to raise feed for his cows.

The Mt. Pleasant congregation was planning a 75th anniversary celebration in 1980. As often happens, choosing the date for the celebration involved an arbitrary decision. Even though there were Mennonite settlers at Fentress as early as 1895 on the one hand, and the building was not erected until 1910 on the other, it was in 1905 that the congregation was recognized by the Virginia Mennonite Conference. So the church council recommended using 1905 as the date of beginning.

The new settlement received a mighty boost from a pioneer who arrived in 1909. He was A. D. Wenger, and he moved there from Lancaster County, Pennsylvania, because, as his son Amos remembers, "He couldn't stand rocks and he did not want to raise tobacco." A. D. Wenger became a promoter of the Fentress colony and sent out an invitation to other colonists through the *Gospel Herald*. In the issue of March 27, 1909, he wrote:

> Our aim is to build up a congregation of believers who will live separate from the world and will train their children likewise. . . .
>
> It does not appear to be unhealthy here. Cases of typhoid fever are very rare. In one home there was malaria last year. . . . Like seasickness it seldom, if ever, proves fatal. . . . The salty sea-breeze from the ocean only 15 miles away appears to have a germ-killing, health-giving effect.

Wenger shared ministerial leadership with J. D. Wert, but after a short time Wert departed under a cloud of scandal and Wenger carried on alone until 1922 when he was called to Harrisonburg to serve as administrator of Eastern Mennonite School. Abram Buckwalter remembers him as a stern man who seemed to think it a sin to smile or be idle. "If he saw you playing at all he gave you something to do." But Mrs. Wenger was a motherly type whom Buckwalter recalls with special affection.

A recent congregational directory showed 16 Wengers among the active membership, a little less than 10 percent of the total of about 200. They are exceeded only by the Millers. A Miller patriarch is Ira whom we found living with his invalid wife, Maggie, in a house built for them in 1915. Ira and Maggie have three sons, 15 grandchildren, and 24 great-grandchildren. He reported that all their descendants except three granddaughters are living not far away. "They drop in and bring us a cooked meal about every other day."

Ira remembered that in the early days "folks more or less skimped along. Even the native people did not live on a high scale. But the church stuck together and worked together." And to confirm Abram Buckwalter's memory of A. D. Wenger as against idleness, Ira recalls that Wenger once "gave a sermon on 'the best way to make a living.' He felt that for the success of the congregation we should support ourselves and provide for the family."

Ira perceives a strong sense of congregational solidarity in terms of interest in him and Maggie. "For the last two years there hasn't been a day that somebody wasn't in." Indeed, even the Mormons got the message. "A Mormon disciple came here and reported that 'my partner told me there is no need to go in there. Those people are Mennonites.' "

Abram Wenger also remembers the old days, though not as far back as Ira. He has lived and farmed here for more than 50 years. "As a farming community, this ranks with the best. You raise two crops a year. In 50 corn crops, never a failure. If there is a problem, it is with too much moisture. The winters are chilly, but not so cold. I broke snow trails only twice in 50 years.

"We never look down on anybody. (Our elevation is about 13 feet.) We get all the atmospheric pressure there is. We have a pleasant neighborhood to live in. We have a lot of black people and they are all good neighbors."

A strong sense of congregational tradition pervades at Mt. Pleasant. One senses it in the ongoing concern for leadership. There is a history of strong leaders at Mt. Pleasant. As Ira Miller tells it, "A. D. Wenger was here as preacher until he went to Harrisonburg in 1922. That's when Brother Clayton Bergey was ordained by unanimous vote. (His wife had voted for Charley Warfel because she did not want to vote for her own husband. When they told her everyone else had voted for Clayton, she withdrew her vote.) At 73, Amos Wenger still serves the Mt. Pleasant congregation, along with district Bishop Philip Miller, Pastor Robert Mast, and Deacon James Bergey, grandson of Clayton.

A multiple ministry is specified in the Mt. Pleasant constitution, adopted February 26, 1979, on a trial basis for two years. "The *ministry* of this congregation shall normally consist of two pastors, at least two deacons, and the district bishop. Other ministers in the congregation may be recognized as pastoral assistants as needed."

Philip Miller favors the multiple system. "We have discovered that one pastor can minister to a certain segment, and another to another. As long as the two interact well, it goes okay." Newcomer to the congregation Jon Mumma agrees. "I appreciate that at this church we have three pastors instead of one. You get a little from each. Amos can minister to the older. Philip to the in-between, and the younger people can identify with Robert who does not wear the plain clothes."

Until recently, no minister received more than token support for his services. But when Robert Mast was called he began receiving approximately half a salary, although he indicated the work of the church took most of his time. For the rest, he reported owning rental apartments and doing some short-term construction and repair work. He also had another business venture in planning. The Mast family lives in a new house which he built himself, and the Bergey dairy provides free milk and eggs.

Amos Wenger has a fruit orchard and was for more than 30 years principal of the congregational school. Philip Miller operates a cabinet shop. "My problem has been to divide my time between the business and church work. I have devised an emergency system. If the church had an emergency, I took off time from the business. If the business developed an emergency—backed up orders or a shortage of cash—I eased up on church work."

Robert Mast, who grew up at Mt. Pleasant and came back after service at several other places, is generally comfortable with a ministerial team. He occasionally finds it a little frustrating to share the preaching. A series on 1 Peter took nearly a year. But he concedes that he is stronger in administration and counseling. One special assignment that falls to Robert is counseling young men who develop a conviction against military service and want to get out. At the time of our visit he was in contact with David Lawson, a navy volunteer assigned to the aircraft carrier *Independence*. David had married Mary Hershberger, a Mennonite girl from Indiana. While visiting in her home congregation in January 1979, he heard Elno Steiner preach a sermon on peace and the message reached him.

The *Independence* was in Norfolk when we were and David took us on a visit of the ship, 1050 feet long by 250 feet wide, roughly the size of 3½ football fields. The *Independence* has a 38-foot draft and can come into Norfolk only at high tide. Forty-nine hundred men are needed to operate the carrier. David had been a radar specialist, but after he had submitted his application for conscientious objector discharge, he was transferred to supply systems.

There is a procedure for obtaining an honorable discharge

on the basis of conscientious objection to violence. A part of
this is to receive endorsements from others to validate this
belief. A memo from Robert Mast to David's commanding
officer read in part: "Recently David Lawson contacted me
regarding the conscientious beliefs in objection to war and
military service that have developed in his thinking and
belief in the recent past.... Serious reflection ... has
brought him to the point of considering his enlistment in the
United States Navy a mistake.... He has stated to me that
should war occur, he would not be able to participate with
the military system in releasing death and destruction on
other human beings."

Mt. Pleasant is a thrifty church. They meet in the original
auditorium, built in 1910. Ministers have served without
pay, and they get their family worship guides free from the
Radio Bible Class.

In one area the congregation allows itself to become ex-
pansive. Mt. Pleasant has its own school for grades 1-10 with
three teachers and 50 pupils. Begun in 1941, the school was
directed for 30 years by Amos Wenger. I asked him how he
devised a curriculum. "Oh, just like the public school," he
replied, "except that we added Bible."

Most Mt. Pleasant families send their children to the
school and other pupils come from outside. Merlin Miller,
who attended for two years and whose son now directs it,
said, "Academically, I think it's A-1. I think all our students
who go [from our school] to public schools are academically
ahead. I think our teaching system has been excellent."

Robert Mast, however, is concerned that the school takes
half the congregation's annual budget of $70,000. "The prob-
lem is, the congregation is operating an institution. We do
not send as much support to churchwide efforts as I would
like."

Mt. Pleasant Christian School includes Grades 1-10 with three teachers and 50 pupils.

It is not that Mt. Pleasant has no interest in the promulga-
tion of the gospel. For many years a delegation of men has
gone to the local jail every Sunday morning to interact with
prisoners about the Lord. Other efforts include services to
the Tidewater Detention Home. Also at home in the congregation is Harold Buckwalter, director of the Virginia
Mennonite Board of Missions' Ministry to Seamen. As a
representative of the church, Harold boards merchant ships
from Taiwan, South Korea, and Japan. "I introduce myself
as a minister and tell the sailors my church has sent me to
welcome them to the port. I lay out a New Testament, then
show a map of the city of Norfolk. Invariably while I am
showing the map, someone will pick up the Testament.

"In the first contact I make every effort to get them off
the ship with me. Many are eager to get to a supermarket. If
possible, I bring them to our home for a meal. These are the
ones who keep on writing. During a trip my wife and I made
to South Korea, Taiwan, and Japan we met 27 of our
friends." Under Harold's predecessor, there were a number
of baptisms and the organization—as it were—of a congregation at sea. Harold always makes baptism available to
persons who make a Christian commitment, but none have
asked for it.

The Mt. Pleasant congregation has also begun to bring
people into its own close fellowship. Sometimes they marry a
member and then later join the congregation. Linda Yoder
followed this route. Linda spoke to Bill Byrd, a writer for
Currents, a local Sunday magazine, about her satisfaction
with the Mt. Pleasant congregation. "It's a wonderful Christian fellowship. When I had a sick child, everyone in the
church stood behind me. When we have problems, everybody pitches in to help."

Jon and Julie Mumma, parents of two small children,

found the Mt. Pleasant congregation the right one for them at a given point in their experience. Julie was a Mennonite from Pennsylvania, Jon a converted drug addict, formerly from New Jersey. They met at the Rock Church, an independent charismatic congregation in the Norfolk area, where Jon had found the Lord. Julie had earlier visited Mt. Pleasant, but it seemed too conservative; Jon likewise. But Julie found the charisma of Rock Church overwhelming, so they settled for a time at Community Chapel.

"Then we got tired of the large church and visited back at Mt. Pleasant," said Jon. "I saw there had been a change. Maybe part of it was in me. I still have a lot of hangovers from the charismatics and I think our church needs a little more verbal praising of the Lord. I like the a cappella singing, but a piano would make it possible to have special music."

But Jon and Julie are drawn by the close community at Mt. Pleasant. Though Julie is somewhat concerned by the complex of family relationships, "we don't have any family here," Jon affirms "the close fellowship, the idea of community. I had a hard time understanding this peace thing. I am a temperamental fellow—but this is one specific thing the church is helping me to understand. The idea of a network of Mennonites throughout the world, a whole world of Christians, thinking of Mennonites in Russia—this has opened me to the idea of peace and nonresistance."

The Mt. Pleasant church was sponsor of a refugee family from Laos. We had dinner with them at the home of Harold and Rose Bergey. The family is Vane Keo Savang, his wife, Nhoun Keo Savang, and their four children. The congregation had found them a house, helped get a job, and given them a Moped for transportation. After two years in a Thai refugee camp the Laotians seemed most grateful for the new opportunity and were faithful attenders at the church even though they understood very little English.

Is the Mt. Pleasant congregation able to hold its young? Surely there are some disgruntled children of the church. Every congregation has them. But we were impressed by the large number of Ira Miller's descendants in the area. And we met four generations of the Bergey family at Mt. Pleasant: Titus, son of the patriarch Clayton; his sons Byard and James; four sons and a daughter of James': Harold, Leonard, Floyd, Lynn, and Joye, and Harold's 18-month-old son, Philip. All of the working age Bergeys except Harold are employed in the family dairy business: 71 Guernseys provide milk for a dairy store at the farm and for two delivery routes. One hundred acres produce forage for the herd and 75 percent of the grain. A two-crop system is used: rye in the fall, and corn in the spring. The land is considerably more productive than Titus remembers from his youth when it "was so poor that a neighbor planted corn in five foot rows, two feet apart in the row."

Both Harold and Leonard have been away from the area and have returned with wives—Harold with Rose from Pennsylvania, and Leonard with Elsa from Harrisonburg, Virginia. Leonard had spent two years in Ghana as an overseas missions associate with Mennonite Board of Missions. What did he accomplish in Ghana? He recalls one accomplishment—"helping people find a way to get oxen to do more than simply plow by arranging for the use of carts with which the oxen could be kept occupied longer."

What was it like to come home? "I came home sick with hepatitis so there was at first no pressure to interact with other people. By now I am happy to relate to this church again. I felt the church had grown while I was gone—in togetherness and in a freedom I did not experience before."

The feeling was evidently mutual. Leonard and Elsa were elected as youth sponsors.

Harold had been particularly pleased to have Leonard come home, for he was ready to leave the dairy business for a position as biology teacher in a local high school. He was also Sunday school superintendent at Mt. Pleasant.

"The health of the congregation will depend on its ability to accept people of other backgrounds," said Harold. "In a sense this is in tension now. There are no black families among us. Some would be uncomfortable with this. This congregation can be a little clannish."

Indeed, with 17 Bergeys, 16 Wengers, and 39 Millers almost any congregation would seem "a little clannish." But an opening has been made. And the leaders have affirmed their dedication to the work of God. "I have praised the Lord many times for the renewal movement which has swept across the church even though I have not been able to absorb everything," said Philip Miller.

And Amos Wenger observed philosophically, "It seems that change must be in the plan of God."

4
Of Many, One

St. Paul wrote in Galatians 3:28, "There is neither Jew nor Greek, there is neither slave nor free, there is neither male nor female; for you are all one in Christ Jesus." I have believed this and sought to follow it, but I think I never saw it illustrated more graphically than in the North Tampa Mennonite Church, on the western coast of Florida.

"How many separate cultural groups are there in your congregation?" I asked Doris Horst, and we began to compile them: Spanish, Italian, Vietnamese, Honduran, Puerto Rican, Pennsylvania Dutch. From here on we became less certain, but surely a 60-member mixed congregation would have a few English and/or Irish. This cultural diversity is a strength in the mind of former pastor Martin Lehman, though also a potential weakness. The weakness, in part, is a matter of self-image. "My feeling is that its perception of itself is as hopelessly divided. Somehow it must come to see that its diversity can be a strength."

North Tampa is also one of the most geographically scattered congregations I have ever experienced. They are distributed throughout the greater Tampa area and on out into

the country. A number of families live as far as 20 miles from
the church building, some as far as 40 miles from each other.

The congregation has a complex history. It is a merger of
two churches, missions really, Ybor City and Ida Street,
located only a few miles from each other and begun in the
late twenties. (The *Mennonite Yearbook* date for North
Tampa is 1927.) Ybor City was the more distinctive of the
two since it was located in a compact Latin American community. Also, Ybor City had Sharon School, a church-
sponsored private school staffed by administrators, teachers,
and Voluntary Service workers, principally from the North.

The compact Ybor City community broke up through the
passage of time and the incursion of urban renewal. Though
the church and school buildings remained, the constituency
was scattered and bringing children to school was an increasing burden. Staff members too were harder to get as they
served for a minimum allowance.

So in 1962 Sharon School was closed and there is still
resentment in Tampa about the closing. "It was a good
school," said Julio Valido, "until a deputation came from the
North and closed it down because there was not enough
growth in the church. Today when anyone comes from the
North" and he looked directly at the editor of the *Gospel
Herald,* "I tell them to go back where they came from."

Martin Lehman, who at the time of the school's closing
was a bishop—the administrator on location—acknowledged that "the closing of the school came as a
tremendous shock to our whole system in Tampa." But he
observed also that operating the school had given Ybor City
the image of a children's church. "There were baptisms, but
as the years moved along, most of the children left. The
church and all the workers were involved so deeply in the
school that an effective adult ministry was minimal. Ida

Julio Valido   Barbara Batchelder

Doris Horst

Roy Horst: "If we can just get ourselves together, we can bring in a lot of new people and strengthen our feeling of family togetherness." Doris Horst: "We ended up with chairs [in the new church], but it almost tore us apart. Yet we really make use of our chairs." Barbara Batchelder: "I am concerned about numbers, but quality growth is more important."

Dominga Moctezuma

Roy Horst

Vietnamese refugee mother and child. Special Sunday school classes
are held for them, and they attend faithfully. Julio Valido: "I finally decided the Mennonite Church taught more Bible than the Presbyterian,
so I joined the Mennonites." Dominga Moctezuma: "I never joined because of the rules. But then the church changed the rules and I joined in
1965."

Street people were also drawn into the school. We would find ourselves all tied up with it and it hampered our work with adult education."

But Sharon School has had results in the long run that few anticipated. Though many who grew up in it left for other Christian traditions, some came back as adults and are now members of North Tampa congregations. Belinda Fernandez is one of these. "My mother sent me to Sharon School because they would babysit me until 6:00 p.m. When I was growing up I wanted to be a Mennonite and wear a white cap. But it was really the love that I craved. When Tito and I were married we went to a Spanish Baptist Church, but Tito couldn't stand the Spanish, so we came here."

Julio Valido was also a pupil at Sharon School. "I was kicked out of public school in third grade because the principal spanked me and I told my mother. She beat up the principal and they had to call the cops. So I went to Sharon School." How did he become a Mennonite? "My father was Catholic, my mother was Baptist, and I was Presbyterian. I went to the Presbyterian Church on Sunday and the Mennonite Church on Wednesday night. I finally decided the Mennonite Church taught more Bible than the Presbyterian, so I joined the Mennonites." He also married one of the teachers at Sharon School.

The churches from which North Tampa came were missions with the budgets supplied and rules set by people outside the area. Now North Tampa is an independent congregation in the Southeast Mennonite Convention. It raises its own budget and sets its own rules. In early 1980 it was seeking a pastor.

What has brought this diverse group together? Not all went to Sharon School. For many of the others it was a response to Mennonite caring. Richard Peterson, one of the elders, said, "What drew me to the Mennonite Church was the love and concern for a new person." He and his wife, Beverly, were also impressed by former Pastor Arthur Wise's willingness to try to answer their questions. ("Where does it say in the Bible that you can't wear makeup"?)

"I grew up a Catholic," said Beverly Peterson, "and went to boarding school. I asked questions, but could not get answers. Arthur Wise tried to answer our questions, so that is why we responded."

For Barbara Batchelder it was the Ezra Beachys. "I didn't know anything about Mennonites except that I expected Ezra to have a beard and a black hat. I kept watching Alice who dressed 'peculiar' but helped everybody. She kept my daughter Penny for me and invited me to a fellowship meal. Then she asked me to go along to church. I came from a small Baptist church and when I entered the Ybor City building I felt right at home."

Her husband, Jimmy, was not a Christian, but he was the kind who would help anybody. He helped with the construction of a new building for the congregation. Roy Horst talked to him and Jimmy made a Christian commitment.

Tom Cannella's story is a little more complex. Tom grew up in New York City and at the age of 10 went to the Mennonite home of Harold Landis in rural Pennsylvania for two weeks under the auspices of the *Herald Tribune* Fresh-Air Fund. Tom and the Landises liked each other and when two weeks were up, he got permission to stay longer. In fact, he stayed the rest of the summer. In later years he began going as soon as school was out. Every summer was spent with the Landises, and the Stumptown Mennonite Church. Later he went at Christmas and after he married he took his wife. But

Tom's family was Catholic and it never occurred to him that he might become a Mennonite.

When Tom and his family moved to Tampa he thought there was a Mennonite Church in town, but never got around to looking it up. Their family attended a small Catholic church which then met in a civic center and seemed to need them. However, "one Sunday morning my wife, Mary, was sick and I decided to go to some other church—I don't know why—so I looked in the phone book and here it was. I went to the church at 9:00 a.m. and found I was an hour early. (I went by Pennsylvania church time.) But Bob Blauch was there turning up the heat, so I waited for the service. The next week Mary went too."

In due time the Cannellas became members at North Tampa. Their daughter Rose Marie at first resisted. But later she came too and eventually found her husband, David Brenneman, in the church.

The Cannellas had friends in New Haven, Connecticut. Tom had met Al Esposito in Tucson, Arizona, when both were in the air force in the forties. The two families kept in touch and when Al in New Haven heard that Tom was buying a lot in Tampa he said, "Buy me one too."

The Espositos were shocked when the Cannellas wrote that they had become Mennonites. But they were liberal minded and willing to come and see. After they themselves moved to Tampa they went along to a congregational retreat and later they too became Mennonites.

Some members at North Tampa are the only ones from their families. Other families are represented by more than one generation. Melita Rivers was a Mennonite from Honduras who moved to Tampa and transferred her membership. She lived with her daughter Lily Lind, who joined in part to support her mother. But now she herself is a loyal member of the congregation and includes in her assignment grading of lessons for Home Bible Studies.

Dominga Moctezuma has known the church since 1934. She remembers early pastor, J. Paul Sauder, and his wife, Alice. Also Anna Kauffman and a more recent deacon and his wife, Amos and Martha Ramer. The Ramers moved to New Paris, Indiana, but their friendship was so strong that Dominga was invited to the wedding of Ramers' daughter. "They put me in the wedding party."

For thirty years Dominga only attended the church. "I never joined because of the rules. But then the church changed the rules and I joined in 1965."

Her husband, Frank, refused for a long time, but as Dominga put it "we worried and prayed" and on January 26, 1975, *Proclamation,* a publication of the Southeast Mennonite Convention, reported that "Frank Moctezuma, age 86, has invited the Lord into his life and has come through his second operation well."

Their daughter Merci married a nonchristian who would not permit her to become a Mennonite. But then he lost his accident insurance and learned that if Merci joined the North Tampa church, they could all get coverage under Mennonite Mutual Aid. Merci was baptized and moved into the work of the congregation.

The same fellowship and caring that brings people into the congregation sustains them in times of crisis. The Charles Forrys moved to Tampa from Pennsylvania because he was a carpenter and got tired of "freezing his fingers." They became supportive members of the congregation and in a family emergency the church supported them. Three of their sons were in an automobile accident and Dale was injured critically in the head and required emergency surgery.

"Our church might have some hard times and some

faults," said June Forry, "but when this accident happened, they really came through. It was Sunday evening and I called the church and Barbara Batchelder and Mary Kathryn Brenneman came to the hospital and sat with me. The church was scheduled to have preparatory service, but they just prayed and cried together. "At the hospital I was told that Dale probably wouldn't live through the night. But they went ahead with surgery which took until 4:30 in the morning. Almost the whole congregation came and sat with us in the waiting room.

"Dale recovered. He has a mesh plate and cannot play any contact sports. Also his interest span is not as long as it would have been. Otherwise, there is nothing wrong with him. It's a miracle. The neurosurgeon wouldn't believe it."

The North Tampa congregation erected a new building in the early seventies, dedicating it in September 1973. Constructing and moving to the new facility produced strain in the congregation, as often happens. The first issue was finding a location. I heard various reports on this. One person said it was put where the pastor wanted to build it. Ezra Beachy remembered that "a lady had land for sale and wanted a church to be built on it. She was pretty fussy about what church it would be and got some literature on Mennonites. She was well satisfied except for the acceptance of black people, but she was able to adjust to this."

Martin Lehman said, "We took a map, pinpointed every family and chose a place that was centrally located, had good access, and where the price of land was tolerable."

Pastor Arthur Wise was made general contractor for the new building. According to Richard Patterson, this was not the best use of his time. "We made a mistake by assigning our pastor to direct the construction of the church building. Then he couldn't work at building the congregation."

There were other issues. One common to many congregations was whether to use pews or chairs for seating in the new building. "We ended up with chairs," said Doris Horst, "It almost tore us apart, yet we really make use of them."

Certainly the effect of the building project was not all negative. Doris Horst remembers moving into the new building as a highlight in the congregation's history. "The church worked together," she said. "We built it ourselves."

Several persons expressed concern to us about the downswing in the congregational life in connection with the new building. "I think our church went through a recession when we moved to the new church, but I think it's picking up," said Charles Forry.

Barbara Batchelder responded, "It seems there is something under the surface. We just need to be able to forgive and forget and once we can do this, we will grow. I am concerned about numbers, but quality growth is more important. When we can work together, we shall grow."

Congregational growth was on the minds of many. One of the problems they face is mobility. People leave because their work calls them elsewhere. Doris Horst said, "If we had all the people in our church that we have had since we came here, we would have close to 200."

North Tampa continues to reach out to people. They were relating to three families from Vietnam. They had not sponsored these families, but became aware of them after they were in the area. Bob Grove, a graduate student at the University of South Florida first got in contact with the Vietnamese, and the congregation was able to provide a variety of supporting services. Included were helping to find houses and helping to repair and furnish the houses. The youth group gave money toward the purchase of furniture. Then the Mennonite churches of Sarasota wanted to help and sent a truckload of furniture. Bible lesson materials were obtained and special Sunday school classes held for the Vietnamese. They attended faithfully.

Like Paul in Ephesus, the North Tampa Mennonites have "a wide door for effective service . . . opened . . . and there are many adversaries" (1 Cor. 16:9). One of the adversaries to be overcome is the stereotyped notion many people have about Mennonites. As Mary Cannella observed, "When people hear 'Mennonite' they are afraid to come to church. It takes a lot longer than for Baptists or Catholics." But she acknowledged that the distinctiveness is a strength. "People go more because of what they believe."

Roy and Doris Horst have been workers at Ida Street and North Tampa since the early sixties. They moved to the area under adverse conditions. Roy was a farmer in York County, Pennsylvania, but came to Florida to recuperate from a kidney ailment. They decided to locate near Tampa instead of Sarasota since there were already a lot of Mennonites at Sarasota. In 1980 Roy was head elder, a member of the church council, and teacher of the Vietnamese men. Doris taught third and fourth grade in Sunday school and together they served as youth sponsors.

"The Lord brought us here," said Doris. "I know He did."

I asked Roy about his dreams for the North Tampa congregation. "My greatest anticipation is growth. I sense there is a tremendous opportunity for growth. If we can just get ourselves together we can bring in a lot of new people and strengthen our feeling of family togetherness. Our people want this, but we have little problems."

A few days earlier, Julio Valido had put it as follows: "Our church has fantastic potentials if we will just use them."

And Martin Lehman said, "It is one of the most challenging congregations. I left it with grief."

5
The Church Behind the Levee

At Des Allemands, Louisiana, people used to attend the Mennonite Church in relays because the building would not hold them all at once. Today there is room for all who wish to come to Des Allemands' new building, but swing shifts in daily work keep some away on Sunday morning. So the congregation provides regular meetings three times a week so that those who cannot attend on Sunday morning may worship on Sunday or Wednesday evening.

The history of the Des Allemands congregation can be read in its buildings. John E. Wenger, who was pastor there for 40 years, remembers the first one acquired in the thirties. "We bought it from the Presbyterians for $200. It cost $80 to move it across town, and $300 for the lot. It was a small building, only 16 x 24." A new and larger building went up in 1950 and soon after this 14 people were brought into the church. An annex was added in 1960 in time for the wedding reception of Joyce Comardelle and Stanley Mecum.

The latest construction was done in 1978 when five volunteers from Indiana took down the 1950 building. Ninety percent of the material from the old building was

Justine Verdette, 95-year-old Des Allemands member.

used for a larger structure in its place. A youth group from Kidron, Ohio, put the shingles on the roof. The rest of the work was done by Des Allemands members using plans drawn up by Gerald Beadle and John C. Wenger. The old church came down just after a meeting of the Gulf States Fellowship in early May 1978. The first service in the new building was held on October 22. They told me with a straight face that they had put up a 150-seat building complete with pews for $45,000!

Across the street from the church lives Justine Verdette, a French-speaking lady in her nineties. She observed the building of the new church during the summer of 1978 and was so impressed with the harmony and lack of swearing that she asked to become a member of the congregation. So Virgie LaValle, a French- and English-speaking member at Des Allemands, interpreted between Justine and Pastor Robert O. Zehr as she gave her baptismal vows. Things like this really do happen at Des Allemands.

Des Allemands (the expression is French for "the Germans") first heard of Mennonites about 1918 when a few families moved in and began farming. Among them were the Chester Wengers, parents of John E. Wenger and Mabel Wenger Hackman. The little settlement lasted only about four years. It was an unfamiliar climate, there were problems with flooding, and the horses got spinal meningitis.

So the Wengers moved to Pennsylvania, but they never forgot the half dozen or so French people who had found the Lord and who remained in their minds as sheep without a shepherd. They came back in 1936 to build a church. The Chester Wengers came first and were followed in six months by their adult children: John and Esther Wenger and Lester and Mabel Hackman and their families. Lester was against the move at first, Mabel remembers, "but the Holy Spirit dealt with him one afternoon while he was alone. Our goal," she said, "was just to come and live among the people. We had a lot to learn."

It was the Dutch among the French, for although the town may be Des Allemands, the dominant local culture is Acadian French and, of course, Catholic.

"What accounts for the church you have here?" I asked Mabel.

"It's just the Lord at work," she said, "where the Book is opened. We came from pretty strict preaching. I do not know, I guess just loving people, visiting. We don't visit enough. I was thinking this morning about the last three people who were baptized in the church. The Lord just brought them to us when they were ready."

Financially, the early years were lean ones for the missionaries, but they survived by gardening and sewing for others. Indeed, it was a lean period for most in the area. Fishing and trapping were the mainstays. Today fishing and trapping are not forgotten, but there are good jobs in the greater New Orleans area. Members at Des Allemands work in chemical and fertilizer plants, grain shipping, railroading, and public utilities. Sidney and Mae Comardelle own a fleet of barge-pushing tugboats.

A modest looking place, Des Allemands is actually quite expensive to live in. Apartments rent for more than $300 a month, and a building lot, if it were available, might cost as much as $40,000. The problem is that much of the surrounding land has been bought by oil companies and is not available for building.

Water is the most pervasive common topic in Des Allemands. It is not like the common stereotype which Joyce Mecum protests—"Are the houses on stilts?"—but this is because the railroad bed serves as a levee and behind the levee the water is kept down by canals and pumps. Rains as heavy as ten inches are common, but the pumps are adequate for these.

Yet the water is always there and though houses are now built on concrete slabs, no one digs basements. Graves, too, are in vaults above ground, for otherwise, they would fill with water and the caskets would float.

Des Allemands is beside Bayou Des Allemands which connects Lake Des Allemands and Lake Salvador which is ultimately connected to the Gulf of Mexico. The water of the bayou is not seawater, but it is affected by tides. (Bayou is a Choctaw Indian word meaning "slow moving body of water.")

One effect of the coming of Mennonites to Des Allemands was to put some life in other churches. "There were hardly any churches here when we came" said Lester Hackman. "The Presbyterian Church had a man who would come on a circuit. The Holiness Church was almost dead. We revived them!"

This might sound as if there were bad feelings between churches in Des Allemands. If so in the past, this is not true now. Pastor Robert Zehr reported a recent breakthrough in interchurch relations. A ministerial alliance was formed which brought together ministers from Assembly of God, Baptist, Catholic, Mennonite, Methodist, and Presbyterian congregations.

Throughout the history of the Des Allemands congregation, the Catholic cultural and religious system has been an adversary. Almost everyone in the area, if not a former Catholic, had parents or grandparents who were members of the church. The Des Allemands Mennonite cemetery is a large one for a small church with a short history. Many of the burials were of people who rebelled against the Catholic

Former pastor John E. Wenger (standing) behind present pastor Robert O. Zehr; Eugene Arsineau, whose genealogy goes back to contemporaries of Evangeline (in striped shirt).

Church and/or who confessed faith in Christ and joined the Mennonites late in life.

But this too is changing, for the Catholic Church is changing. (Perhaps the Mennonite too.) "My husband's two sisters are Catholic," said Denise Hotard, "but they go to the prayer meeting at the Baptist Church. They would never do this before. Now they invite you to the Catholic Church. Before, they didn't want anybody who wasn't Catholic."

The pastor of the local Des Allemands Catholic Church is also friendly. "I thought for a while we were going to convert him," said Judy Beadle, "when he came to see the new church. There had been a large offering and he could hardly believe that we had this large an offering in a church the size of ours. When we had the dedication, Robert included him on the program." John E. Wenger agrees with the greater openness to other denominations. "I don't care if they don't leave the Catholic Church as long as they see Jesus." He observes too that "the Catholic Church is changing. They have a sign in the front of their building 'I have decided to follow Jesus.'"

Des Allemands, however, is a Mennonite church with a 40-year Mennonite tradition. The Des Allemands Mennonites know themselves as Mennonites and support the worldwide mission of the Mennonite Church. Though of modest size, they are the largest in the nine-congregation Gulf States Mennonite Fellowship. Their pastor, Robert O. Zehr, is moderator of the fellowship.

It was a strange new experience to call Robert Zehr as pastor at Des Allemands. John E. Wenger had been their first and only pastor for 40 years. His son John C. Wenger, treasurer of the congregation, took leadership in helping them see that they had resources to support a pastor and the Robert Zehrs came from Kansas. A number in the congregation already knew them since they had served earlier at Madisonville on the opposite side of Lake Pontchartrain.

The older Wengers and the Hackmans remain, however, and continue to participate in the congregation. "We like Brother John," said Virgie La Valle. He's still 'Rev' to me. Whenever I need him, he comes. I like Brother Zehr too. I was sick. I called him and he came and anointed me."

I asked Robert Zehr what is required to be a Mennonite at Des Allemands. "To confess faith in Christ and be baptized," he replied. "We teach all the things that other Mennonites teach: nonresistance, the Mennonite confession of faith. We are a bit flexible on this. If some say, 'I can't swallow this,' we work with them. We ask, 'Are you willing to work at what Jesus is saying?' We do not require that persons be 100 percent in line to work with them."

As in any "gathered" church, not all who begin in the faith, continue. There are many relatives in the Des Allemands Mennonite Church. In a few days I could not begin to get the relationships clear—but there are also many families only partially represented. As in other Mennonite communities, some go away to school. Joyce Comardelle Mecum was one of these. I asked her why she came back after attending Hesston and Goshen colleges. "The church, I guess. Also family ties." The return was supported by her husband, Stan, who came from a place in northern Indiana and vowed he would never go back there.

"My rebellion," said Joyce, "was going off to school. Then when I did that I was ready to come back!"

Sometime in the past decade Des Allemands had a bad experience, some sort of congregational crisis. No one said clearly what it was, but Joyce described it as "the problem. We dropped down to one Sunday when there were only about 30 in the church and I thought, *Was this the end?* But then we kept plodding on and now it has built up again."

One who left was Eugene Arsineau. "I grew up in the church. There was a period when I left. I met Audrey and I started going to the Catholic Church with Audrey."

Why did he leave?

"I guess because they had a 'hassle' in the church and I was not mature enough in my faith to understand. Some who had been in the church from the beginning left. Some years later (in 1976) we asked if we could go along to one of the church conferences. Marion Bontrager was there and we enjoyed his talks—but more the way he acted. So we came back to the church."

Eugene asked the editor of *Gospel Herald* for more articles on Mennonite history and doctrine, more teaching on conscientious objection to war. "At times I feel far apart from the Mennonite Church. I went to Hesston, Kansas, once and there were five Mennonite churches in one town! I want to visit Goshen some time, and also Pennsylvania."

I made the mistake of suggesting to Robert Zehr that Des Allemands is the end of the line. Without becoming violent, he pointed out that Des Allemands people are in touch with the wider Mennonite Church. Church leaders stop in the community going to and from Central and South America. Members of the congregation can identify denominational leaders.

Like any congregation, Des Allemands people see room for improvement. "We would like to see people who left come back," said Judy Beadle.

"The congregation hopes to fill the building," said Robert Zehr. "There is no feeling to tear down this building and enlarge it as they did with the last, but rather to have a second congregation in the area." Indeed, he dreamed a little more expansively. "There should be several Mennonite

'witnesses' in New Orleans to a point where there may some
day be a Provident Bookstore to serve the area."

I thought about the Des Allemands building in its place
behind the levee, with its comparative safety from storms
provided by pumps which can deal with a ten-inch rain. The
congregation, too, is a sort of place of protection where
people can come for help when the problems of life get
them down. This is an old figure for the church, truly, but at
Des Allemands it seems more than usually appropriate. Like
the town of Des Allemands, things may be a little soggy at
times, but basically tranquil.

Frank and Kathy Bachteler are charismatic Episcopalians

**Sunday school pupils at Des Allemands Mennonite Church: Travis
Martin and Vonnie Bergeron.**

who began attending Des Allemands after Frank's work brought them into the area. "We have adopted them," said Robert Zehr.

Frank put it another way. "I have visited a number of churches, but here they live their religion."

Virgie LaValle appears to be an unofficial local missionary for the congregation. Virgie has outlived two husbands and is now married to Harry LaValle, her third. A woman of influence in Des Allemands, she owns eleven apartments on the street named after her, "Virgie's Ct." "Since she's a Christian, she's been bringing a lot of people to the Lord," said John E. Wenger. (For a good many years she was not.)

One of those she brought was Felix, an old man a doctor asked her to care for, since he wasn't expected to live more than three months. But with good care he lived nine years and after an operation on his eyes was able to walk around the community.

"Later," said Virgie, "he asked to be a Christian. He said to me (in French) that he wanted to get his spirit right with the Lord. I said to Harry, 'Felix wants to be a Christian. What shall I do?' Harry said, 'Call Brother John. He'll know what to do.' So I did and he said, 'I'll be right over!'"

When we met Harry LaValle he was a retired project director-engineer for Hooker Chemical Company, who was still called in occasionally for troubleshooting. Harry had wandered into Des Allemands late in the 1960s and discovered Virgie. In due time she took him to church and they were married.

Harry was a baptized Episcopalian but "I didn't go to church until I married her and I have gone ever since. Further, I have gotten all mixed up in the work of the church. These have been the best eleven years of my life."

Behind the levee.

6
Through South Texas

"Two weeks after we came to Houston both the children got pneumonia and people in the congregation were most supportive. During the first four months I got to church about one fourth of the time, yet I was made to feel at home." In this way Betsy Shoup described the ministry of the Houston (Tex.) Mennonite Church to her.

Betsy was one of 15 earnest persons from Houston Mennonite who met with us one evening to talk about what it means to be a part of the 60-member congregation in a city of 1½ million that is growing by more than 100 persons a day. We found this congregation in a reflective mood: the pastor, Marlin Kim, had resigned and they were doing a self-study before calling another.

Houston was the first stop in a five-congregation sample of the south Texas Mennonite scene. Of the five congregations visited, two had pastors in the process of leaving, three used Spanish as the chief language, and two had dual conference membership. Only one of the five was more than 30 years old. One congregation had ample Christian education space, but only two children. All but one are "mission" churches, drawing part of their support from a sponsoring agency.

This will be a congregation by congregation survey, looking for similarities and differences, and seeking to paint an authentic picture.

"Who are the Mennonites and what in the world are they doing in Houston?" asks the introduction to the fall, 1979 *Directory of Houston Mennonite Church.* "These two questions arise again and again. To answer these is somewhat like trying to explain the meaning of believing, living, caring, sharing, or serving. Indeed," the introduction goes on, "these elements are the basis for the Mennonite faith and the foundation for the Mennonite heritage."

The Houston congregation began in 1967 as a mission related to the Western District of the General Conference Mennonite Church. Its first pastor was Elmer Friesen who served for three years. He was succeeded by Marlin Kim who was about to leave at the time we visited there.

As part of the self-study, Houston Mennonite prepared a congregational profile. They found that 23 percent of their active participants drive more than 20 miles to church, 34 percent are 30-40-year-olds, 20 percent are of Hispanic origin, and there is a wide divergence of educational experience.

Thirty percent were Mennonites before coming to Houston, 32 percent belonged to other Protestant groups, 33 percent had no affiliation, and 5 percent were Catholic. There is considerable turnover at Houston Mennonite. More than 300 persons have been members over a 12-year period, but seldom more than 50 to 60 at one time.

What brings people to this congregation? Carl Dube had never heard of Mennonites before he met and married Louise, a Mennonite from La Junta, Colorado. "To me it is just the concern and support of a small group that makes it a family when you don't have your family."

Jim Emmert agreed. "I'm a single person. You have to identify with what family you have. This is the only family I have."

Linda Kim moved to Houston after marrying the pastor's son, Ray. "At first I couldn't stand the singing because I came from the Lindale Mennonite Church which has the best singing in all Virginia. But now I feel at home. I was a member for two months when they made me secretary of the board."

Not everyone who comes to Houston Mennonite finds this combination of family and responsibility satisfying over the long term, according to Marlin Kim. He has served as a hospital chaplain, and "quite a few have come to the church through the crisis ministry. The problem, however, is that it does not seem to be permanent." When the crisis passed, interest in the church has tended to wane. "The longer it goes, the harder it is to get them involved."

I asked about the congregation's dreams for the future. Terry Shoup responded, "The fact that Houston is growing and that we are the only Mennonite Church in the city gives us a chance to share the Anabaptist vision and I see us doing this. I can't say what all this will be. It's a matter of responding to the opportunities God gives us."

Frank Seena, a Hispanic member of the congregation, said, "I think the history of this congregation speaks for itself. It has really struggled quite a bit and yet we are still standing. I think the critical thing is that we all stand together."

Houston Mennonite is affiliated with both the Mennonite Church and the General Conference Mennonite Church. Why this double billing? As much as anything, they said, in

Houston Mennonite meetinghouse, the only Mennonite church facility in Houston, a city of 1½ million people.

order to be listed in the denominational handbooks of both groups. In this way more people may become aware of their existence. The Houston Mennonite meetinghouse is located on a (relatively) quiet suburban street. Its sign announces boldly "Church of the Sermon on the Mount." As of this writing, there is plenty of room for persons who wish to search together for the meaning of that sign in a city of 1½ million people.

Two hundred miles away is Corpus Christi, a smaller Texas metropolis than Houston, but also busy in oil, chemicals, and international shipping. In Corpus Christi, we visited the Prince of Peace Mennonite Church, Paul Conrad, pastor. Paul was scheduled to leave Prince of Peace the following summer, so our coming provided an occasion for him to reflect on his work in the Mennonite churches of south Texas over a period of more than 25 years. In a few months this would be ending.

Paul and his wife, Ann, came to Mathis, Texas, in 1953 as Voluntary Service workers—he as a builder, and she as a teacher. "We did house building for people who lacked facilities," he recalled. "They got the material and we provided labor. We designed a basic two-bedroom house and devised a way to manufacture cement blocks. Later we began to charge $400 per house for our living expenses."

The mission activity among Mexican Americans at Mathis went back to the middle thirties. But pastors came and went, and by about 1950 Elvin Snyder, a former Argentine missionary, was teaching at Alice, Texas, and commuting to Mathis, 35 miles away to hold services. One Sunday only three were present and Elvin recommended to Mennonite Board of Missions that they take the work seriously or close it down. The response was to send in service workers. A building unit was organized along with recreation, crafts, and kindergarten. A unique feature of the Mathis service program was a three-bed maternity hospital. From 1954 to 1963, 1,800 babies were born there.

The service program seemed to give impetus to the building of the Calvary congregation in Mathis and today there is a membership of 148 there, plus young and middle-aged Mexican Americans who moved from there to other parts of the Mennonite Church. Paul served as pastor at the Calvary Mennonite Church in Mathis from 1957 to 1969, and in 1970 was assigned to the Prince of Peace congregation in Corpus Christi.

Paul was involved in the design and construction of the church buildings at Mathis and at Corpus Christi. Both structures have been visited by hurricanes. In 1961 Hurricane Carla came to Mathis on a Sunday. "I had never experienced a hurricane before," Paul recalled, "but someone came to warn us. We had our regular morning services and throughout the day the wind kept getting stronger. I told people that the church would be open for any who wished to come and by 6:00 p.m. it was filled with 200 people. By 8:00 it was really packed. We continued a church service until midnight.

"It was great satisfaction to realize that we had put up a strong building, and I felt secure. I remember telling people that the steel in the structure of the building is like faith in our lives. We do not wait until the storm comes to put in the steel. The same is true with faith."

Nine years later just after the Conrads came to Corpus, on August 1, 1970, Hurricane Celia took the roof off the church building. Mennonite Disaster Service repaired the church and did other repairs in the area, continuing until January 1971.

It is easier to get some people to church during a hurri-

cane than at other times. In the months and years following
Celia, Paul would visit people and invite them to church.
"Some would say, 'when there is another storm, I will be
there.' "

We met some of the members at Prince of Peace. Among
them was Ninfa Salinas, who found Christ as a teenager at a
Mennonite Brethren Mission in "the valley," the phrase
they used in Corpus to refer to the area along the Rio
Grande River. Later she married and moved to Corpus
Christi where she has attended Prince of Peace since 1964.

Services in the congregation are bilingual. Since everyone
I met could speak English, I asked occasionally about the
importance of Spanish. Ninfa responded: "Living so close to
the border we need to know both languages."

Carmen Reyes came from a Catholic background "but
not fanatic. I just grew up saying 'I'm a Catholic.' " Then
ten years after her marriage, her children began to attend
Prince of Peace. They said, "all the others had mothers there
but they, so I went for their sake and I'm glad I did."

What are your hopes for the congregation? I asked her.
"Growth and peaceful brotherhood—and a new building.
Three classes in one room is too much commotion."

At the Reyes home we met Carmen's daughter Sylvia,
who spoke of the Mennonite Youth Fellowship, and how it
might be improved. "I would like to sing in MYF." She
spoke also of the trip they took as a group to Waterloo '79,
the youth convention of the Mennonite Church held in Waterloo, Ontario. The evening before I had visited MYF
following their work project and heard the sponsor,
Raymond Gutierrez leading the group in a consideration of
Philippians 3. Seeking to be candid about his own life story,
Raymond told them, "I did a lot of things when I was young
that I now regret."

Ninfa Salinas, who found Christ as a teenager in a Mennonite Brethren mission, along the Rio Grande River.

The Prince of Peace meetinghouse in Corpus Christi, Texas, 200 miles south of Houston.

It was a full weekend at Corpus. We talked with Lupe Garcia about the state of the south Texas Mennonite churches. "There has been growth in some churches, not in others. While the Spanish congregation at Premont was closed and the Anglo is reduced in numbers, we have opened a new congregation at Matamoros, Mexico." I noted in the bulletin that on the following Sunday, Lupe was scheduled to preach at Prince of Peace on the theme, "Church Growth—A Deliberate Commitment."

Will Spanish come back in Corpus? "Not likely. In a small community such as Mathis, it can be maintained, but here the young people don't want to learn it."

We met Frank Ortiz, Sunday school superintendent and church council chairman. Frank and his wife had been Nazarenes, but the Spanish congregation they attended closed down and the Anglo Nazarene congregation did not seem to have a place for them. So they moved to Prince of Peace. They were impressed to find an Anglo pastor speaking Spanish.

Frank supports a bilingual approach in the congregation. There was a strong movement to have the new pastor be a Mexican American, but as Frank observed, "We will still have to be bilingual because most of the youth want to learn English. A minority wanted to change our church to be completely Spanish, but we say we need to keep English for the sake of the Anglos."

So on Sunday morning I sat in the bilingual Sunday school class. Though on a long-term basis I think it would be tiring, as a single experience, it was interesting. But I will never know what those Spanish-speaking class members behind me were saying.

I talked to Lupe Longorria about the work of the South Texas Mennonite Council since he was the immediate past president. "The South Texas Mennonite Council serves as a mini-conference within the South Central Mennonite Conference," he said. "As time goes on it will become more important because of the distance from Kansas. The conference is geared toward larger, more stable congregations whereas congregations in the council need frequent contact and counseling. There is the potential to form a separate district conference, but because of the need for subsidy, we are not likely to separate within the next five to seven years."

What is the vision of the council for the eighties?

"We are working on church growth. Also, we will have to make adjustments to inflation as it relates to subsidies. We will have to deal with the military draft again, the issue of nonresistance, the economic advantages of the armed forces."

On Sunday evening we went to Robstown, 20 miles away. Pastor Gilberto Perez was a Mennonite who had come from Mathis. His wife, Elizabeth, was a Methodist from Brownsville. They met in a factory in Archbold, Ohio, and became active members of the Spanish Mennonite Church in that area. After study in a Bible Institute, they were assigned to begin a Mennonite congregation in Robstown and had been there for six years. "We came with the addresses of two people," said Gilberto.

Except for a few interpretative comments for us, the service at Robstown was all in Spanish. Though there was much we did not understand, we felt welcome and involved. Did I detect, however, that the 30 people present understood more English than they implied? It seemed to me at one point that Gilberto was calling (in English) for only Mary and me to stand so that he could introduce us, but the whole audience stood.

The singing was a cappella and was interspersed with eloquent sounding remarks by most of those present. Some spoke more than once. After an hour or more of songs, prayers, and testimonies, I was invited to address the group with Elizabeth as interpreter. Then Elizabeth took the children out for stories while Gilberto preached from Isaiah 6. At the end he gave an altar call (which he explained to us in English was for persons who wished to give their lives more completely to Christ). Most of those present went forward. As we left, we greeted each other with "God bless you" which I took to be the Spanish Mennonite equivalent of the holy kiss.

Monday evening we called on Robert and Ruth Reist who told us about the United Mennonite Church of Premont. Robert's father, H. Frank Reist, once president of Goshen College in Indiana, had moved to south Texas for his health, locating eventually at Premont. He was the first pastor of the Mennonite Church near there. Bob grew up in the area, found a wife at Goshen College, and operated a dairy farm until 1961 when he became a high school science teacher. Though we found Premont a pleasant place, with fresh garden salad in early February, farming in the area is precarious because of the fickle weather. Bob told us the average rainfall is 23 inches a year, but half of it may come in a single rain. One year there may be as little as 10 inches; another year may have 50.

He took us to see the meetinghouse of the United Mennonite Church, a merger of the Mennonite Church in the country and the Mennonite Brethren congregation in town. United Mennonite belongs to both conferences and the mode of baptism is according to individual preference. The two congregations merged not only their members, but also their buildings. The MC building was moved to town and joined with the MB building. The former serves as auditorium, the latter as Christian education and fellowship wing. Alas, there is little need for the Christian education space. "We have no children here" said Bob. Then he remembered a high school girl and one fourth-grader. "There is not much to keep young people in Premont," he said.

The Reists told us about their four children who support the church wherever they are, but not in Premont. There is John, who owns ten acres and works for a rancher in central Texas. David is a nurse in Akron, Ohio; Susan a factory worker in Goshen, Indiana; and Curt a draftsman in Hesston, Kansas. Bob gave similar accounts for the six children of Samuel Swartz, pastor at United Mennonite.

They told us too about the Chapel of the Lord, the Spanish Mission which had functioned earlier in Premont. Beginning in 1960, the Reists had supported this effort and opened their home to a group of young men who came to the mission and joined the Mennonite Church, then scattered from Premont like the rest of the young Mennonites. One of these is Chuy Navarro and he was the subject of our last Texas interview. But first we visited Pastor José Calderon at Mathis.

Mathis, according to the Texas tourist guide, has a population of 56,000 and "is a commercial center featuring livestock and cotton, also producing large quantities of grain sorghum, flax, and varied truck crops." To us Mathis did not appear quite as prosperous as this description would imply. But then an area is generally not at its agricultural best in midwinter.

Pastor Calderon showed us the meetinghouse and told how when he arrived five years before, most in the congregation were 55 and older. Now, he said, there are 15 to 20 younger families. The answer to church growth, he said, is "prayer and fasting. My father-in-law fasts the week around. I teach the congregation that the work of the church is not just my work, but belongs to all of them." As we talked, one of the newest members strolled by and told us in English, but with Latin eloquence, how Christ delivered him from dependence on marijuana and heroin.

Pastor Calderon chided us gently for visiting only him. "Come again," he said, "when you can meet the whole congregation. Too many church leaders," and he named several, "come to visit me, but the congregation does not get to know them."

The final contact in our south Texas survey was with Jesus (Chuy) Navarro in San Antonio. One of Robert and Ruth Reists' "boys," Chuy met us in the office where he works as an administrator in the Texas Department of Human Resources. He recounted the various stages of his developing experience in the Mennonite Church.

Influential in his early life was Richard Fahndrich, who became pastor at the Chapel of the Lord in 1960. The pastor before him was a solo leader, but "the Fahndrichs introduced church organization and the Reists supported it. So I was given little tasks—usher, Sunday school teacher, superintendent. I played the piano, became a member of the church council. The Fahndrichs were excellent models and drew quite a few young men into the church. They saturated me thoroughly with Mennonite doctrine."

When the Fahndrichs left in the mid-sixties, Lupe and Seferina de Leon were sent from Mathis as a young Mexican-American pastoral couple. "It was a new experience to have a young Latin pastor with whom I could interact about the Christian life and think—instead of being told—about what was right and wrong. It was time to move from being spoon-fed to a new phase."

This new phase began to find expression in agitation for an organization to represent potential younger leaders in making decisions about the work of the Latin Mennonite churches in south Texas. The result was the South Texas Mennonite Council and Chuy became the first chairman. Under his leadership the council was a force to be reckoned with, but eventually he resigned and direction passed to other persons. As he talked about the council and its possibilities, he seemed like an old war-horse with the smell of gunpowder in his nostrils, but his work at the Department of Human Resources had him in other harnesses.

As I had with a number of others, I asked Chuy about the importance of Spanish. "Among the elderly Mexican Americans," he replied, "Spanish is God's language. For outreach you definitely need Spanish. For instruction in doctrine, young people and children prefer English. It works well when you have a combination of Spanish and English."

With all this emphasis on Spanish and Spanish culture, I inquired whether I would be welcome at a Mennonite Church in south Texas. "There is never any problem for Anglos to affiliate with Mexican-American congregations," he said. "Snowbirds [winter visitors] come to Brownsville in droves."

But I think if I were looking for a place that seemed to need me, I would go to Premont. The United Mennonite Church has a great deal of room for visitors.

7
Spanish and English Spoken Here

At Carlsbad Mennonite meetinghouse the English service is at 9:00 a.m., and the Spanish service at 11:15. Some attend both, as well as the Sunday school in between. One bulletin serves for all. The Spanish congregation is one of the more recent ways the Mennonites in Carlsbad, New Mexico, have sought to be relevant to their area.

Two Mennonite families came to Carlsbad in 1964 and 1965 for health and job opportunities—and to build a church. "We had allergies," said Ernie Good, "and we wanted to move to the Southwest for our health, also to be useful in a smaller congregation. We considered Fresno, California; Albuquerque, New Mexico; Spencer, Oklahoma. While we were thinking about it, Jason and Miriam Stoltzfus contacted us. They were ready to move to Carlsbad and invited us to locate there too."

The climate suited them just fine, and employment opportunities opened—though Ernie first went to barber college to learn that skill. (When I was in Carlsbad he cut my hair and Mary was well-pleased with his work.) Building a congregation was a more complex undertaking.

In Carlsbad, New Mexico, the Mennonite meetinghouse serves two separate congregations, one Spanish and one English.

A peaceful looking small city of some 20,000, located at 3,010 feet altitude on the bank of the Pecos River from whence comes its water, Carlsbad, New Mexico, is not always as peaceful as one would hope. When we were there in early February, our host reported that there had been three murders since the first of the year. In the middle sixties Carlsbad was not especially waiting for Mennonites. "This is a very conservative town in terms of patriotism," said Ernie. "Southern Baptists are strong in the area and are very militaristic."

"We tried various things to introduce ourselves: *Choice* and *Heart to Heart* radio programs, and Home Bible Studies without much response. The town is pretty well 'churched,' especially the Anglos."

Yet organization of a congregation proceeded apace. They became part of Rocky Mountain Mennonite Conference and by September of 1966, they called a pastor, Paul Stoltzfus. Paul is no longer pastor, but remains in and supports the congregation. "I'm a church 'starter-upper,' " he said.

An economic recession in Carlsbad related to a decline in local potash mining probably made possible their purchase of a church building. They obtained a moderate-sized church building for $24,000 from a group that could no longer use or hold it and they looked toward filling it. Though they have not brought into the congregation as many of their fellow townspeople as they hoped, they made a home for Mennonite refugees from other parts of the United States. "Our congregation is mostly 'transplanted' Mennonites," said Pastor Peter Hartman. "It is a milder climate favorable for people with respiratory problems and it attracts them." If the climate attracts such people, the congregation also reaches out to them.

Among those attracted by Carlsbad Mennonite were John

and Esther Hodel who moved there permanently in 1974 after spending the two previous winters in the area. They stopped to visit once while traveling to Texas as Esther recalls, "and felt the love of this congregation. John said, 'we're going to live here.' " John died in 1976, but Esther continues in Carlsbad though she has children in other parts of the country. "It's a small enough congregation that it's just like one big family. It was so before my husband died, but now that he is gone, they take care of me. I was asked why I stay here. One reason is the climate, but another is the congregation."

Esther, a retired medical doctor, still sees patients occasionally in her home. One specialized group of clients is German-speaking Mennonites from Seminole, Texas, 100 miles away. Esther's husband was German and she speaks the language.

The Marvin Kenagys were young farmers in Missouri, but Mrs. Kenagy became greatly restricted by rheumatoid arthritis. So they moved to a ranch near Carlsbad and her health improved so that she was able to function as a ranch wife. Marvin was the first practicing Mennonite farmer I had met on the trip since leaving Chesapeake, Virginia. I discovered that farming in New Mexico is done on a different scale than in the better watered East. "It takes 75 acres to sustain one beef cow," said Marvin. He has 150 head, so that means a ranch of more than 10,000 acres.

Then there are the Nelson Histands, who came from Mississippi because of his heart trouble and the Leon Eashes who left Indiana because of his asthma. Eashes first went to Phoenix, Arizona, but it was too hot there. Then they lived for three years in nearby Tucson, which was also pretty hot—and expensive. Finally they came to Carlsbad and found the climate moderate and the prices reasonable.

Recent comers at the time of our visit were the Harold Reebs, who had disposed of their assets in Illinois and came to Carlsbad to stay.

Elsie and Ruth Martin moved to Carlsbad from Albuquerque. Elsie teaches nursing in the local state college, and Ruth cleans houses. "The church is bigger here than in Albuquerque," said Elsie. "It's more stable. There we cleaned the church building during the week. I was Sunday school superintendent, taught a class, was church treasurer, led 'the opening.' We have a lot of capable people here, a lot of older people, but they are very capable."

The Carlsbad Mennonites believed in publicity, especially as the congregation was beginning. Richard and Laura Rhodes came in response to a report in *Christian Living* magazine which invited Mennonites to Carlsbad. They were open to an invitation. Richard was from Virginia and Laura from Iowa. They met at La Junta, Colorado, and had decided they wanted to live in the Southwest. They took a vacation to look for a place, came to Carlsbad, and before they left had bought a house. Later Laura's parents, the Sylvan Yoders, came and found that Sylvan's arthritis did not bother him here as it had in Iowa, Texas, and Florida. "Also, we got pressure from the kids."

Throughout most of the history of Carlsbad Mennonite, there has been a Voluntary Service unit in the city, sponsored by Mennonite Board of Missions with encouragement from the local congregation. There was a general agreement that the overall results for the congregation have been positive. "I get a lot of comments downtown about the contribution of VSers to the area," said Peter Hartman. "They wish more churches would have such programs for young people." In the early years, the VS unit helped to make Mennonites known in Carlsbad.

"We would hear people asking about individual unit members after they left," said Ellen Good. "Mennonite Board of Missions has considered phasing out the Carlsbad unit, but nobody here wants to hear of it." To demonstrate the interest in and appreciation for VSers, the congregation includes them in its fellowship and program and each one is provided with a host family during the period in Carlsbad.

We spent an evening with the VS unit. There were seven of them. Norman and Vera Helmuth were retired farmers from Ontario, and there were five young women: Gail Smith, Harrisonville, Missouri; Rose Gonzalez, Corpus Christi, Texas; Donna Fahlstrom, Hot Springs, Arkansas; Diane Hinkle, Ft. Wayne, Indiana; and Lara Leichty, Wayland, Iowa. Members of the unit worked principally in social and medical services. Some were paid and some were not, but in line with Voluntary Service practice, all wages were contributed and each person received an allowance.

Voluntary Service also feeds the congregation, for some have stayed in Carlsbad after Voluntary Service. Lee Eash, who cuts hair in Ernie Good's barber shop told me, "We were in VS here and I think this is one of the friendliest churches I experienced. We just stuck around."

The Carlsbad church reaches out in other ways. The weekend of our visit we learned of their plan to sponsor a Vietnamese refugee family. A house was waiting for the family, they were collecting clothes, and that week a picture of the family had arrived.

On Sunday morning Pastor Hartman read excerpts from a letter from the city of Wichita Falls, Texas, thanking the congregation for help after the tornado that devastated sections of that city in the spring of 1979 and inviting them to come for a visit. The pastor acknowledged that much of the work referred to had been done by Leon and Edna Eash.

On Sunday evening he read a petition opposing the liquor license of a local grocery store, and invited those who wished to support this effort to sign it. And Rose Gonzalez was circulating a petition calling for the city to provide bicycle lanes.

But probably the most far-reaching recent extension move of the Carlsbad Mennonite Church was to participate in the opening of a ministry to Spanish-speaking people. "We had one Spanish family who took a backseat in our congregation," said Peter Hartman. Then "Stanley Weaver and José Ortiz came to help us think through our situation. They recommended a separate Spanish congregation." Funding for the Spanish effort comes from outside. Carlsbad helps principally by making their building available and giving general encouragement. Members of the Spanish group are invited to potluck meals. The Spanish pastor is a member of the church council. The Spanish church is called Iglesia Evangelica Menonita.

The pastor is Raymundo Gomez, who with his wife, Clara, and three small daughters moved to Carlsbad from Archbold, Ohio, though he had grown up in Mexico. He told me that he was formerly a Presbyterian and went to a Presbyterian Seminary, but the Presbyterians had no place for him to serve. The Nazarenes would have used him, but he got to know Mennonite pastor Conrado Hinojosa at Brownsville, Texas, and was attracted to the Mennonite Church.

I asked him how he had begun his mission in Carlsbad. He reported that he tried door-to-door contacts at first, but the Jehovah's Witnesses use this method and he does not wish to be identified with them. It is hard to get people to understand that although they both oppose the military draft, Jehovah's Witnesses and Mennonites are far apart in beliefs. So now he works from family to family—one contact

Raymundo Gomez (left) and Peter Hartman. Raymundo is pastor of the Carlsbad Spanish congregation, and Peter of the English.

leading to another. He also broadcasts in Spanish from a local radio station every Saturday morning. "I hear comments about the broadcast in my barber shop," said Ernie Good.

I asked Pastor Ray about his long-term goals for the Spanish congregation. He responded with three:

> (1) To teach the people what the Bible and our church say about our basic doctrines. Too many say, "We are Mennonites," but don't know why in the same way that others might say, "We are Catholics," but don't know why.
> (2) To take care of the growth of new believers in sanctification. It is important that all know what they believe to protect them from strange doctrines.
> (3) To tell the people that we appreciate the help of the Anglo church, but we need to try to take our own responsibility as soon as we can. We need to be responsible not only to receive help, but also to give.

Though they have not been able to build their church locally as they would like, the Carlsbad Mennonites take satisfaction from certain opportunities for service they have had. Ellen Good observed that "there have been some contacts with persons who were brought to the Lord, but most seemed to want to go back to the denomination they knew formerly."

Paul Stoltzfus came home from a weekend away and got a distress call from a woman whose husband gets drunk and beats her. Marilyn Hartman was intensely involved with a person who seemed to be seeking courage to look life's problems in the face.

There are those among the Carlsbad Mennonites who expect the church to begin growing more locally as well as continue to draw people from other parts of the country. Richard Rhodes is one of these. He dreams of the Spanish

church becoming large enough to form its own separate congregation. Also, "I envision our own church becoming 150
members. I think we will have more impact on Carlsbad in
the next ten years—people know us better. They know what
we stand for."

On our final evening in Carlsbad, Jason Stoltzfus, one of
the founding fathers, asked me a question to which I could
not give a clear answer. He wondered whether in the
churches we had visited along the perimeter of the United
States there has been less inclination of the children of Mennonite families to embrace the faith of their parents than in
the large communities in the heartland.

I assumed from this that a number of youths from the
Carlsbad congregation have cast their lots with other Christian traditions—or none of them. I could only respond that I
had indeed observed a moving in and out of a number of the
congregations along the way. I recalled for him the
experience at North Tampa where church leaders closed
down a school because it did not seem to build a church.
Later on former students of the school came back to the
church as adults. I suggested that the results of our efforts
are not always immediately observable.

We noted that probably it is more difficult to pass on our
faith to children in an area such as Carlsbad sparsely popu-
lated with Mennonites and many miles from the nearest
Mennonite congregation. But I was conscious too that living
in a large concentration of our own kind is no guarantee that
the children will accept the faith of the parents.

We talked about the closed Mennonite communities in
some areas where it is assumed that the maturing person will
be Mennonite whether or not he or she has a personal faith
in God. We agreed that an open society with a gathered
church, where there is opportunity to accept or reject one's

own tradition is more desirable than this. But we were pensive nonetheless, because we believe in our Mennonite tradition with its simpleminded devotion to the Bible and would like to see it spread both at home among our families and abroad.

It snowed the night we came to Carlsbad. Not a big snow, but enough to make the streets immediately slippery and to cause some auto accidents. But before noon the next day the snow was melting and filling the streets with water, because Carlsbad has no storm sewers. Nor do the houses have gutters, I noticed later. Evidently there is so little precipitation, they are not considered necessary.

Nobody complained about the snow, though some were a little apologetic, for they wanted us to have a good experience in Carlsbad as a place of mild and pleasant climate. They welcomed us as I am sure they do others, and no doubt would have urged us to stay longer, even permanently.

What does Carlsbad Mennonite expect of its members, I asked Elsie and Ruth Martin. "They don't push you," said Ruth. "But they generally include you in everything."

8
An Arizona Sampling

"Tucson is the largest city in the world that gets its water supply from wells alone," said James Wenger, pastor of the Shalom Mennonite Church. "The water table is dropping. Some say that by the end of the century we will run out of water. Others say it will last four to five hundred years."

The possibility of water shortage came to be furthest from the minds of the people of Tucson and Phoenix, Arizona, the week we were there. Some said the storms which visited the area were the worst in 500 years. From what we learned, the results were mainly annoying for Tucson. For Phoenix, they spelled disaster. Indeed, sections of the state of Arizona were declared a disaster area by the U.S. government.

Though we learned of one Mennonite family of the Phoenix area who left their home because of high water, our visits to these two cities were little hindered by the flood. However, the storms continued for days after we had left Phoenix and gave an ironic twist to Arizona's image as a sunny paradise. At a motel in Prescott, Mary heard a tourist from Minnesota complaining bitterly about the rainy weather. "I'm going back to Phoenix and will get the first flight home to Minneapolis."

There are eleven Mennonite churches in the greater Phoenix area. In addition to Tucson, we contacted four of these eleven: two on our trip through Arizona, and two on an earlier visit to Phoenix. Thus what we have learned cannot be held to be fully representative of the Phoenix area Mennonites. But none of these reports is claimed to be fully representative.

The Shalom Mennonite congregation at Tucson is a merger of two former Mennonite groups with divergent priorities: one had a strong emphasis on evangelism and the other was stressing community, even community of goods. In the middle seventies neither one was reaching its goals satisfactorily, and on March 5, 1978, the two groups merged.

Since they had represented diverse emphases, they began carefully and first of all developed a congregational confession of faith. All went well until the time came to choose a name. A minority held out for avoiding the use of the name "Mennonite" and instead using a name like "Tucson Community Chapel" to make it easy for people to identify.

So the issue was decided by vote and "Shalom Mennonite" won out, a name Pastor Wenger had submitted but did not really expect to be accepted. "We get lots of comments about it," said Kathy Leichty, one of the charter members of the congregation. Some associate the name with Jews (not surprisingly) and one person called because he wanted to refer a Jewish-Christian couple to them for fellowship and nurture.

A Voluntary Service unit works alongside the church and this, too, takes some explaining. Said Renee Giovarelli, "I find myself defending the VS idea. Some think it's cultish." A common assumption seems to be that Mennonites are associated with or similar to Mormons who are well known

Jess and Dorcas Lara: "We enjoy the fellowship [at Shalom Mennonite]. It's like a family."

in the Southwest. James Wenger said jokingly that he looks forward to the day when people will hear of Mormons and say, "Oh they're like Mennonites."

The Shalom Mennonites seek to cover both ends of Anabaptist concerns—evangelism and peace witness—and identify with other groups in the city who have these interests. Sometimes it is hard to combine the diverse emphases. For example, just before our visit, a Leighton Ford evangelistic campaign was held in Phoenix, and Shalom Mennonites were identified as participants with a recognized contingent in the choir. About the same time an anti-draft rally was held at the University of Arizona and some of them were in it. "I wonder what John Sheaffer [Leighton Ford's advance man] would think if he saw me in that," said James Wenger.

Jess and Dorcas Lara had recently joined the Shalom congregation. I asked them why. "We started attending when we moved back from New Mexico," said Dorcas, "and we lived close to the church building. I was raised a Mennonite and we enjoy the fellowship. It's like a family."

Jess, who was once a Catholic, was impressed by "interaction among all the people in the congregation. It is not divided by age-groups." He was also impressed by "broad interest in the mission and missionaries." Not only a few specialists are concerned, but the whole congregation.

In an effort to put significance into congregational membership, Shalom congregation has prepared a "Shalom Mennonite Fellowship Commitment" which all applicants are asked to sign and which is to be renewed yearly. It covers a wide area and it was reported that after two years a few declined to renew. This means, of course, that their membership in Shalom Mennonite is ended.

Historically, we were told, there has been rivalry between

Renee Giovarelli, Faith Wenger, and Kathy Leichty. The church's name (Shalom) and the idea of Voluntary Service both take explaining.

the cities of Tucson and Phoenix. Tucson was once the capital of Arizona, but this was later moved to Phoenix, which is surging ahead in population. Mennonites are newer in Tucson, and Shalom, the one congregation there, has only a small membership. So they are clearly outnumbered by the multi-churched Mennonite community in the Phoenix area. However, they identify especially with two of the smaller groups there, Koinonia Fellowship at Tempe, and Iglesia Menonita Emanuel at Surprise. The three have a picnic together once a year. It was these other two congregations which we visited next.

We attended a Saturday morning session of the Koinonia Fellowship Church Council. Those present included Stan Roberts, chairman and congregational moderator; Sophie Brown, secretary; Henry Schrock, co-Sunday school superintendent (with his wife, Sandra), and Don Yoder, pastor. Arriving late was Mark Bodenhamer, treasurer, whose house had been threatened by the flooded Salt River the night before. He and the family had moved out to the Roberts home, and in the morning he returned to check on the house. At that time the river was within one fourth mile.

Mark was philosophical about the threat of flooding. "There are certain things in our personal lives which we are working through. Last night during the flood I said, 'Lord, if You want to get it together this way, all right.' I think it's going to be a blessing." The flood alarm was particularly upsetting to two Laotian refugee girls the congregation had just sponsored. The call came at midnight and their elementary understanding of English made it difficult to explain clearly to them why it was important to leave. But the council observed in reflecting on the incident that moving to another family home of the Koinonia Fellowship should help them sense that their sponsorship is broader than one family.

Koinonia, organized in 1976 by three Mennonite couples in the Tempe section of the greater Phoenix area, also has a name that gets attention by being out of the ordinary. "I would not choose 'Koinonia' again," said Don Yoder, "because you have to explain it." But the concept speaks well for what the congregation evidently aims to be: a closely knit, caring community. In addition to the regular Sunday morning program, most Koinonia members participate in small-group fellowships which are reorganized every six to eight weeks. Often these consider different topics and persons choose a group on the basis of interest in the topic. Currently, all groups were beginning a program called "Congregational Goals Discovery Plan" which would take five weeks.

I asked Don Yoder about the significance of such a study for the congregation. He mentioned several rather general advantages of the program: (1) There is the value of all working together on something. (2) It is not expected to be a final statement, but rather a process to help chart a course. It is recommended that a congregation goes through an exercise every three years. (3) It gives everyone a chance to be heard.

One of the goals Koinonia had already set for itself was the purchase of land for a church building. Don expected that this would be reaffirmed in the goal discovery experience. In the meantime, Koinonia worshipped in a Seventh-Day Adventist building, a happy arrangement since the days of worship normally would not overlap.

As at Shalom, Koinonia has a statement for members to sign and to renew yearly. Some hesitate to join because they are not in complete agreement with the congregation's goals or its stand on peace and nonresistance. There is ferment in Phoenix on the peace issue. John Howard Yoder had recently been in Phoenix, and had addressed the Greater Phoenix Evangelical Association. A friend of Don's, who is pastor of an independent church, was greatly interested.

I asked Don about his vision for the eighties. He responded as much in his role as a church planting coordinator (which he is one-fourth time) as the pastor of Koinonia Fellowship. He believes the Mennonites of Phoenix should be planting several new churches in the eighties. "We need one on the east side with us." He gave me a copy of a recently published newspaper article which predicted that the greater Phoenix area will receive nearly 50,000 people a year in the next 20 years. He hopes to see this planting done on a mother-daughter basis—that is with a larger, older congregation relating to the young one to provide fellowship and stability.

Also "the whole peace area is going to be a new frontier force in Phoenix. Koinonia is right next to Arizona State University. I am not sure what we should do." As if in answer to this question, that very afternoon there was a meeting of the New Call to Peacemaking at the Church of the Brethren in Phoenix, but Don was turned back by a flood-related traffic jam on the Mill Avenue Bridge.

Since Koinonia had begun recently, I asked how many people are needed to start a new congregation. "Three or four strong families for a core group," said Don's wife, Bonnie. She said there is need for this core group to provide stability so that you can invite to your fellowship the hurting people, those from broken homes.

Surprise, Arizona, is a town of 5,000 occupying one square mile 10 miles from Phoenix. "Twenty years ago," said Allan Yoder, "it was 20 miles from Phoenix. Observing the changes in their environment, the town council (of which Allan was a member) had annexed 28 square miles to the west of them so they could control the development of this area. Surprise is a borderline community, said Allan. Some of the people look toward the country and work on the land. Others are urban-minded and find employment in the city.

Allan Yoder has been pastor of the Iglesia Menonita Emanuel (Emmanuel Mennonite Church) in Surprise for the past several years. "Our church is in a good position," he said, "because most of our members are among the urbanized group. The way I see it we can stay ahead of the changes." Most of the members live in Surprise, not far from the church building, making it one of the more compact congregations we visited.

As the name implies, there is a predominance of Mexican Americans in the church, though not all. The pastor himself is Anglo (his name betrays him), but we discovered that he was born and lived the first ten years of his life in Cuba, and his wife, Rebeca, is from Costa Rica. When we first met, Allan spoke of his vision for Hispanic Mennonite churches in Western United States. For starters we need churches in these cities, he said: El Paso, Phoenix, San Diego, Los Angeles, Denver, Albuquerque. "Then we can fill in between. We want to start 'Anabaptist' Hispanic churches," he said. "We will need persons with the gift of evangelism and those with the gift of teaching to interpret the traditional Anabaptist doctrine."

The Emmanuel Church is Anabaptist in one sense, at least. It has leadership by the people. There had been a Voluntary Service unit at Surprise, but the unit was closed "as soon as I came. They were doing a lot of things in the congregation. When they left we had to do these things ourselves. By now all of our Sunday school teachers have been Christians at least a year. We have two or three song leaders, a piano player, guitar players."

There are twelve churches in Surprise, four of which have significant Hispanic ministries. "Our church is the only 'bilingual' congregation among the four though some of the others teach some English in their Sunday schools. We have a very defined ministry to people who are 'going some place' and who are willing to get into the church and help."

I did not get to see a constitution for the church, but I learned that leadership is through the elders of whom there are three: the pastor, along with Carlos Carbajal, Hispanic; and David Rice, Anglo. Carlos taught the Sunday school class the morning we attended. The text was from John 1, and Carlos noted the humility of John the Baptist who considered himself unworthy even to untie the shoes of The Teacher to come. Carlos observed that under the old system a disciple was expected to do everything for a teacher but untie his shoes. "We have a new system," said Carlos, "where we are called to serve one another." (Carlos taught alternately in English and Spanish.)

The sermon also was in two languages and the theme was "Our Covenant with God." In a mimeographed handout and in his English remarks, the pastor stressed the importance of keeping our covenant renewed, up-to-date. "We all need a covenant renewal periodically. It leads us to become more committed to God."

One reason for the importance of keeping our covenant current is to be clear on our identity so that we can speak to others for Christ and our church. "We speak to people about the church and they say, 'What church?' We say 'Mennonite Church,' and they say, 'What's that?' We say, 'Oh, we're an evangelical church' or 'We're like the Baptists,' or 'The Assemblies of God,' when the person really doesn't know what the Baptists or the Assemblies are all about, and probably we don't either! We need a covenant so that we can speak out of our own experience. Until we learn to verbalize our experience, in no way can we fulfill the Great Commission." These seemed like wise words and I learned that the sermon was part of an ongoing emphasis by the elders leading toward a proposed statement of faith for the congregation.

The pastor's concern for Anabaptism was somewhat tempered in the area of military service. The problem, he observed, is that many Latin young people in Surprise come out of high school with an inadequate education and no marketable skill. "The military provides them with options: they can get away, learn a skill, come back, and get a decent job. It's a hard problem. I do not know how to work at it."

Surprise is adjacent to Sun City, a middle- to upper-middle-class retirement community in the Arizona desert which has received nationwide attention. It has a wall around it and sterile looking palm trees. You can buy a house there, settle in, and live on your pension in comparative comfort with others of your kind. Since Surprise is something less than middle-class in terms of the size of its houses and the neatness of its streets, I wondered if people in Surprise might resent Sun City.

"Probably they do," said Allan, "just as they would a factory belching smoke. But like a factory, Sun City and Sun City West (its later neighbor) provide opportunity for work. These are retired people who do not work, so they need a lot of services."

The two largest Mennonite churches in Phoenix are Sunnyslope with 219 members and Trinity with 207. Certain interrelationships may be established. Sunnyslope was founded in 1946, and Trinity is a daughter congregation begun in 1963. Don Yoder, pastor at Koinonia, was formerly pastor at Trinity. Other congregations which we did not visit are Berean, First, Grace, Palm Glen, Paradise Valley, Sun Valley, and Sunnyview. It is a pity to have missed these other congregations as several of them certainly would have given a different perspective from the congregations visited. If Shalom, Koinonia, and Emanuel appear to be largely concerned with church planting—getting on their feet— what will Sunnyslope and Trinity be doing? Caring for winter visitors, it appears, mothering VSers, and carrying a disproportionate share of the conference mission giving, since the smaller churches still need subsidy. Also, at times, grieving over the breakup of Mennonite marriages. "Phoenix is a pretty free-wheeling city," said Ray Keim, pastor at Trinity. "People come here to get away from family, so ties may be looser." Some marriages don't hold together. In fact, the incidence of marriage breakup came to the point that the Southwest Mennonite Conference in its fall, 1979 session, took an action of concern about this and in support of marital integrity.

Sunnyslope had recently gone into a new building of modern design. Two former buildings, if I remember, were still on the lot and still in use. One could read the growth of the congregation in the growth of its buildings. The new building was designed especially to be available for winter visitors: its seating was arranged in banks from side to side. In the summer when attendance was smaller, the congregation could retreat toward the center and not feel engulfed in the building. In the winter the group expands toward the wings.

In Phoenix we found the Discipleship Voluntary Service program directed by Mary and Gene Herr and sponsored by Mennonite Board of Missions. We concluded that this is less a service program (although the people we met worked for money in service-type jobs) than a spiritual exercise program

for the participants. Each person was assigned specific readings and evaluation forms to do every week. There was a
weekly meeting of all unit members for discussion of the
readings, and regular retreats. Several of the Phoenix congregations served as sponsors for individual households and
provided host families for individual members.

"I think they are more giving than any congregation I
know," said Greta Yoder concerning the Sunnyslope congregation. "My 'foster parents' have a spare bedroom apart
from the house. They have given me a key and they call it
my apartment."

We went to a Sunday morning service at Sunnyslope. We
sang gospel songs and heard a report from Navaho
missionaries, the Peter Burbanks. Associate pastor Stanley
Weaver was in charge and interviewed the Burbanks. Years
before, he had been a missionary to the Navahos, but retired
in favor of Navaho ministers. Mrs. Burbank told of the problems of Indian women who are Christians and their husbands are not. "At our church there are only two men and
all the rest are women." A filmstrip reviewed some of the di-
lemmas of being Navaho in light of the background of
cruelty and injustice to Indians.

We went to Sunday school class taught by Richard Sho-
walter. There were 40 in the class of whom ten were visitors.
The lesson was on peace and class members shared
experiences and statements on issues related to peace. As
usual in adult Sunday school classes, the time ran out before
the issues were resolved.

We went to lunch with Pastor David Mann, and his wife,
Mona. They talked to us about the Sunnyslope congregation. About making a place for winter visitors. About seeking
to foster community when members are scattered all over
Phoenix. ("We have Sunday school classes with deacons and

deaconesses in the class. Also prayer groups, and Bible study groups within the Sunday school class.") About how some persons come for the winter and want to stay. About reaching out to persons and families who seek the support of the Mennonite fellowship. (Once or twice a year the pastor leads an inquirer's class for persons who are "seekers" or who want to review their faith. It is not required that a person accept baptism as a result of this experience, but the way is open.)

We talked with Stanley Weaver about his half-time work as associate pastor of Sunnyslope congregation ("basically involved with committees and Christian education") and his other half as overseer for the Southwest Conference ("basically functioning on invitation, not as a person who decides program, but as a resource to congregations").

I asked about his dreams for the Southwest Conference. "There is a huge opportunity to plant new churches," he said. "Also, there is a heavy Spanish population. One of my dreams is to see a ministry to Spanish become a significant part of our work."

As a final contact before leaving Phoenix on this earlier trip, we visited Ray and Clara Keim, pastor and pastor's wife at the Trinity Mennonite Church. Ray, who had a background in counseling, told the congregation when they arrived that they were not good in administration, but in "developing people." Clara told us that when they came to Phoenix, "we kind of presented ourselves as a team. Today the congregation evidently perceives me as 'pastor's wife,' a definite role. I think I am basically functioning as a deaconess. I am never elected to any office in the church, so am evidently perceived as already having a role."

Ray spoke of the strength represented by the congregational elders and of Sam and Marie Hershberger, retired

persons who agreed to do some of the administrative work
which Ray claimed he did badly. He told of how the elders
helped him set priorities: not first a counselor, but first a
preacher.

He spoke of being Mennonite in Phoenix. "The Mennonite identity can get a little thin. It was good for us to be
at Waterloo [Ontario, the biennial Mennonite General
Assembly]. However, we did feel when we came that Mennonites here are much more free in revealing their identity.
Christian teachers find each other in school. A strength here
in our congregation is the Mennonite tradition of whole
families going to church. My friend, John Robertson, pastor
of Bethany Presbyterian Church, used to needle me about
nonresistance. But once he preached for us and was amazed
at the number of men present in the service. 'Where did you
get all these men?' he wondered.

" 'Oh, these are conscientious objectors to war who came
to Phoenix to perform alternative service.' He hasn't said
anything to me against pacifism since then."

There are eleven Mennonite churches in the Phoenix
area, but all are moderate size to small. What are they
among so many? At least it appears that Mennonites are
present in sufficient variety that almost anyone who truly
wishes to be Mennonite can find one with a suitable style.
And if the visions of persons we met come to fruition, in the
future there will be more, opening their doors to any who
are willing to take seriously the Mennonite version of the call
to follow Christ and to support one another in the pilgrimage.

Ray Keim, pastor at Trinity Mennonite in Glendale. The elders helped him set priorities: not first a counselor, but first a preacher.

9
Living with Change

Change is the essence of life. Experience is an ever flowing stream. We all know this, but often we fail to see the change because it comes slowly and there are no dramatic convulsions to bring it to our attention.

Two Mennonite congregations in southern California demonstrated for me more than any I had seen thus far the inevitability and persistence of change and the need to respond if the church is to survive. One began in the 1920s (though one member remains who came to the area in 1912) and the other in the 1930s. They were solid, stolid Mennonite churches in rural or semi-rural California. Today both congregations are urban—part of the sprawling complex that is greater Los Angeles—and each continues to cherish aspects of its heritage. But those who worshiped here and are gone would be hard pressed to believe they were on familiar ground. We visited Mountain View and Calvary on the same weekend, in that order, and the reports will be in order of the two visits.

We found the Mountain View congregation involved in what pastor Willard Ressler described as a "grief process," mourning the loss of half the members, having dropped from near 200 to less than 100. The story they told was like this. Mountain View began at the North Pomona Union Chapel in 1934, moved to an abandoned schoolhouse in Upland in 1943, and began to use its own new building on Seventh Street in Upland in 1947. At this point it became known as the Seventh Street Mennonite Church.

By 1968 this building was crowded, so the congregation bought a lot and began to make plans to build. After five years there was a buyer for the Seventh Street building, so they sold it and accepted an invitation from the First Mennonite Church of Upland (General Conference) to use their facilities for a separate worship and joint Sunday school. About the same time the congregation became involved in change of pastoral leadership and its congregational consensus was found to be frail and began to disintegrate.

"There was no major disagreement," reported congregational chairman, Jake Shetler. "We sold our property too soon and were not yet ready to build, so people got discouraged and drifted away. But," he continued, "we have had a definite turn around and now we are on the way." Indeed, the two problems that had troubled them, leadership and facilities, seemed to have been clarified. They had called a pastor six months before and had just poured the foundation for a new church building. In the meantime, they were meeting in the headquarters of the Upland Women's Club since their reduced size could fit into this building.

But the anticipated high cost of the new building (some $420,000) had helped them seek for some way to make better than average use of it and they decided to organize a preschool. This was also seen as a way to provide some income. I wondered how they determined the need for a preschool program. "There are waiting lists for every school around," Shetler said.

We met with Lucy Maust, a member of the preschool committee and with the pastor's wife, Letha Ressler, who had been appointed its director. They explained that a preschool is basically a nursery school, and commented on the "outreach" potential of the preschool program.

"The church sees it as an outreach," said Lucy, "the area of need that is greatest. I personally don't approve of mothers working unless they have to. But I taught school for ten years and I see the need for children to have a good experience. We didn't want to build this building that would cost so much and just have it sit there—even though it will get a little 'beat up.' "

Several persons told us about opposition to the preschool facility from the Upland planning commission because some residents of nearby condominiums did not care to live near a children's facility. But Dale Fahndrich, chairman of the building committee, felt that the plan would be approved. He noted also the value to the church of facing some opposition. "I do feel that some of the experiences we have gone through have tended to act as a cohesive for those of us who have decided to stay."

As for the future, "I would hope that we could find a way to grow and do a better job of reaching people around us than we have in the past. I think many people have 'needs' if you can find a way to meet them."

Jake Shetler agreed. "We are hoping that we can come a long way from where we were 30 years ago when we just sat there. I don't think we can look for growth through families resettling. I don't think that's helpful to the church anymore." As Jake implied, a number of the earlier members at the Upland Church had been refugees from more severe cli-

Dale Fahndrich, chairman of building committee at Mountain View: "I would hope that we could find a way to grow and do a better job of reaching people around us than we have in the past."

mates. One of these longtime supporters is Irvin Brunk. Why did he come to California?

"For my asthma. In Scottdale, Pennsylvania, I had to sit up and sleep in a chair every night from early fall until late spring." So he went out to look for a better climate. He got a round-trip train ticket to Phoenix, Arizona. While there he discovered that for another five dollars he could extend his trip to California. That brought the Brunks to Upland in 1948.

They reflected on the changes in the congregation during their time and decried a seeming lack of church discipline today. "Pretty much everyone does what's right in their own eyes," said Ruth Brunk.

But they agreed that this is a congregation that cares. Irvin remembered the congregation's strong support when he submitted to open heart surgery. Irvin's son Floyd and his wife, Esther, reported the same at the death of their son, David Kim, by stabbing while a student at a local Christian college. "I've never seen so much caring in all my life as at that time," said Esther.

Having heard the story of Mountain View's recent problems, I asked Willard Ressler why he accepted the assignment as pastor. He mentioned several things including "the style of leadership I felt they needed was the style I have to offer—not pushy, but more by example and training." He mentioned also that the call was confirmed by a small group in Indiana of which he and Letha were members. "We had a special meeting of our group the same night they had a meeting here to decide whether to call us. As they had prayer for us, the phone rang and it was reported that the Upland congregation had given a strong vote. I had said that I needed time to make a decision, but the group said, 'Why wait? Tell them yes.' So I did."

He spoke of his concern to help the congregation work through the grief process for those who had left—"I think it's coming"—and about other tasks to accomplish in the congregation. "I am very much interested in relationships. Also, very challenged by the young adult age. We have a nice-size group. One of the things we will be working on is the 'draft' issue. We are going to start out by talking of the meaning of spirituality.

"There is pretty broad support for being a 'Mennonite' Church, supporting nonresistance and separation from the world. One of the things they asked me was whether I could support the Mennonite emphasis. There is quite a variety, but I enjoy variety."

It is 40 miles from Upland to Inglewood, 45 minutes by freeway. Though both were once farmlands, Upland remains suburban while Inglewood is not far from Watts. Some of the lots in Watts are still bare from the burning in the mid-sixties.

The Calvary Mennonite Church in Inglewood is some ten years older than Mountain View, but until the fifties, their experiences were quite similar. Then blacks moved in along with the city. What would Calvary do about blacks?

John David Zehr was pastor of Calvary in the fifties and he railed against racial discrimination. I remember that we published his fire breathing articles in *Christian Living* magazine. But after he left the congregation it was not clear what would happen to Calvary. Some members had moved away and were commuting to the church building. James Lark and Nelson Kauffman wanted Calvary to develop a ministry to blacks in its neighborhood. In 1961 Leroy and Irene Bechler came from Saginaw, Michigan, to lead the congregation in this direction. Their coming was a signal for a general exodus. Leroy remembers that one of his first pastoral duties was to issue about 30 church letters.

"I remember the first Sunday we were there," said Irene. "There was only a handful of people and my heart was down in my shoes. But soon things began to happen."

How did you start to build the church? I wondered. "We became involved in the life of the community. The PTA had disintegrated because the community changed. When we came they were trying to revive it and we helped. The first three PTA presidents became members of our church.

"Our children contacted children. Our son Kent invited Michael Eli and consequently the whole family accepted Christ in a home Bible study."

Later Dorothy Eli confirmed the story from their perspective. "If Rev. Bechler saw a new face, he got the name and address. So he came to call on us and asked if we wanted a Bible study in our home. I think that was the first time I understood salvation. My husband and I and our two children accepted the Lord in our home."

In a paper prepared for a course in church growth at Fuller Seminary, Leroy Bechler reported that "in an on-the-spot survey within the congregation the majority of adults came into the fellowship by personal invitation. The reason they continue as members is because of the love, warmth, and concern that was felt and shown. . . . Another was the fact that the Word of God was taught. It was here where their spiritual needs were met."

Kathleen Richardson seemed to be an example of this. "I came to the congregation really by accident." The church she was attending emphasized appearance so much that she did not feel comfortable there. "Irene Bechler and I had worked together in PTA and my children started attending the Mennonite Church. Then I decided I could go too. After two years I heard Pastor Bechler say 'Mennonite' and I went

home and looked it up. I found it was very old and believed
in washing feet. But everything was so warm and the congregation was concerned about your spiritual life. So once
you get involved you keep on."

In 1970, Calvary congregation made a major change in

**Calvary Mennonite Church and School, opened for business in the fall
of 1970, and still growing.**

strategy that has affected their life ever since. Until then they had worshiped in a small frame building constructed by Mennonite farmers in the 1920s. Now they bought a much larger facility offered by a congregation that had decided to run from racial integration. As George Smoker told the story, a member of this denomination moved to the area from Jamaica. "The pastor received her into the congregation on Sunday. On Wednesday night the board voted to sell the building." It was a bargain, though at $150,000 a large investment for a small congregation.

The new building included facilities for an elementary school and in the fall of 1970 the congregation opened a Christian day school. Nancy Cash was principal at the time of our visit. We talked with her and also viewed the Monday morning opening. There were 231 in the school from kindergarten through sixth grade, and plans were being made to add the seventh grade. There is a Bible instruction program and it is a requirement that all those enrolled attend Sunday school also. "Our emphasis this year," said Nancy Cash, "will probably go more toward parent ministry and make it a requirement for parents to be involved in a six-week seminar as a part of enrollment."

We looked in on one class as the teacher checked the Sunday school attendance the day before. Not all had been there, but Nancy had reported that "we average 112 in Sunday school [that would be about 50 percent of the Calvary school enrollment] and three forths of these are in our own Sunday school."

Not all members of Calvary were completely convinced that the 1970 move into a larger building was the best one. Henry Burmeister, chairman of the trustees, said, "I think that spiritually we lost. There is not the feeling of oneness we had formerly. I don't think the growth has been what was

Nancy Cash, principal of Calvary Mennonite School: "Our emphasis this year will probably go toward parent ministry."

expected. I think we shifted our emphasis to the school."

But later in the conversation Henry affirmed his faith in Calvary's future. "I think there's a lot of potential for the church here. We've got the school program and are in contact with a good many parents. The children are getting a better education than they would in the public school. That the parents are willing to commit their children to a private school shows that they will stay in back of the program."

Sending children to a private Christian school puts pressure on the family budget. "One dilemma Calvary has faced is that in many families, both parents are employed out of economic necessity," wrote Leroy Bechler. "Also, many members are furthering their education which enlarges their opportunities for growth and advancement. This in itself is not bad. However, if priorities are not kept in proper perspective, the local church is hindered from involving and equipping its members for ministry. The Spirit is willing, but many times the flesh is tired."

The school has brought some parents into the church. I talked with Lee Knox, a member at Calvary for three months. "I came here during vacation Bible school and I really like the people. I have a Baptist background and it wasn't that I was leaving my background, but my son goes to school here. Since I'm here I'm getting involved in a ministry with boys."

Richard Reese, a member of the board of elders, told his story. "At 5½ I gave my heart to the Lord. But at 23 or 24 I struck out on my own, though I still had contact with the Lord—tokenism. At 28 or 30 I asked the Lord to give me direction about marriage. I got married, but still did not go back to the Lord."

Later he and his wife decided their child needed to go to a

Pupils at Calvary Mennonite School. It is a requirement that they attend Sunday school.

church-sponsored school. After one unsatisfactory
experience in another school, their application was accepted
by Calvary. "At open house it was explained that Calvary
had a three-pronged approach to education: the home, the
school, and the church. Part of the curriculum was for the
student to attend Sunday school. Several months later we
were notified that we had not lived up to our part of the bargain: Leslie was not in Sunday school.

"I was never for dropping children off for Sunday school,
so I began attending and got engrossed in the lessons. The
teacher would ask me to stay for morning worship, so I
began to do that also. Pastor Bechler had a 'strange' way of
preaching: expository, right out of the Scripture. So the first
Sunday in May 1977 I found myself going to the altar. I
thought I should find out what Mennonites believe, so I
read some of the booklets. I have been working diligently in
the church since then.

"When I made my little prodigal split, I thought Christians had no fun. But I have found that Christians' fun is
much more intense. We are not numbing ourselves with
drugs and so the joy is free to come out."

In 1979, the Bechlers concluded reluctantly that they had
made their major contribution to Calvary and it was time for
the congregation to have new leadership—a black pastor. So
they resigned and withdrew from the congregation in order
not to complicate the task of selecting a new pastor. A pastoral selection committee was at work and Arthur Cash was
serving as interim pastor. "My work was supposed to have
been school chaplaincy," he said. "Now the other is added
on. Until someone else comes, we are running pretty hard."

Dorothy Eli was alarmed by talk that the new pastor need
not be a Mennonite. "I feel if I don't want to be a Mennonite, I can go to another church. The ordinances, the way

they teach the Bible—these I don't want to see changed. If we get a black pastor, okay, but that's not a big issue with me."

George Smoker, a retired African missionary and a member at Calvary affirmed the need for a black pastor. He also showed enthusiasm for the school. "The big challenge and the opportunity at Calvary is the Christian day school. I would see this as a tremendous means of evangelism."

My final contact with Calvary was Kevin Jordan, son of the late elder Charles Jordan, and a member of the pastoral selection committee. He expressed a point of view I had not yet heard at Calvary. "We have been depending on the pastor to do a lot of things the congregation can do. I think now is a time to look at our purpose, to redefine our purpose. I think what has attracted people to Calvary is that it has integrity and some unique things, some of the Mennonite doctrines that have been clouded by culture: (1) nonresistance, (2) sharing our resources, and (3) covenant. The fact that members of the congregation are struggling with these things is new to us. I think this will bind us together and give us some clarity.

"Many who were members at Calvary and some who have left were attracted because of its uniqueness. In an urban setting where life is impersonal and the trust level is not that good, a congregational fellowship is very impressive."

It seems a long way from Calvary in the twenties and Seventh Avenue in the forties to the Calvary and Mountain View congregations today. Yet some remain who have been there and are here. And in spite of cultural battering, I believe the tradition remains—the tradition that the Bible is to be taken seriously and that Christians care for one another.

10
When Radicals Mature

"I don't believe we were ever in a church before that emphasizes the Anabaptist tradition like this one. They even celebrated Menno Simons' birthday." When Velma Mierau moved with her husband, Eric, from Herbert, Saskatchewan, to Fresno, California, so Eric could study at Mennonite Brethren Biblical Seminary, they had their choice of four MB congregations in Fresno. But they chose to attend the College Community Church—Mennonite Brethren in nearby Clovis.

As Eric put it, "What appealed to us was that the church was not as pastor-centered as Mennonite Brethren churches are. For me as a busy student, church is mostly the Sunday service. I thought it would be good to be part of a participating congregation, not an audience." Eric was also impressed by how open the members of this congregation are with each other, in contrast with his experience in a rural church in Saskatchewan where people were more reserved.

The interview with Eric and Velma was our last with members of the College Community Church—Mennonite Brethren in Clovis, California. This was the most academic and professional church we had yet found on our tour of Mennonite congregations. There are 42 teachers in the congregation, we were told, and nine doctors/dentists, plus additional nurses. It was also the most freely self critical congregation. A congregation of individualists, yet holding together and supporting one another. It was known to take in people who might otherwise have left the church altogether, yet it concerned itself more with the Mennonite heritage than other congregations nearby. It had no organized local "mission," yet a dozen from the congregation were engaged in foreign service and many others had at one time been there.

We were warned that this was not a typical Mennonite Brethren Church. We had not set out on this trip to look necessarily for typical Mennonite congregations—just any that we found along the way. So the lack of typicality was no drawback really, but it suggested the need to be careful in seeking to understand this congregation within its Mennonite Brethren context.

The Mennonite Brethren are descendants of a renewal group among the Mennonites of Russia. Disturbed at the lack of spirituality in the Mennonite churches and seeking a more expressive form of worship, a few families organized a separation movement in mid-nineteenth century. Today Mennonite Brethren are known on the Mennonite scene for baptism by immersion, for large congregations, an emphasis on evangelism, and for accommodating more to the pressure of national patriotism than some other Mennonite groups: MB church buildings in the United States, for example, commonly display American flags.

Three out of these four characteristics are not apparent at College Community. There is a baptistry, but no flag and they are not known for evangelism. Rather than seeking for

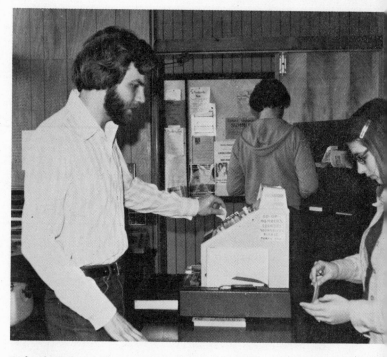

Richard Wiebe of Clovis Community Church: "I see a real divergence between the image of the congregation and the reality."

people, they find people seeking them—and leaving just as freely. Though some may be troubled by the leavings, there is general acceptance of this. Indeed they "commission" them for the new role in another congregation. And they are not a large congregation—less than 200 members, perhaps 120 active.

A common reason for families leaving is the lack of a strong youth program. College Community is an adult-oriented congregation. There is no "young peoples" organization and the Mieraus, for all their positive feelings, reported that the youth class was so unsatisfactory their daughter stopped attending. Other families, however, are not troubled by this lack of youth-oriented activity, for they observe that adults are open to young people and they are pleased to see their youth have opportunity for this personal acquaintance rather than a formal program. Carol Friesen commented that "our 16-year-old enjoys intergeneration activities, but also goes to the youth group at Butler Avenue" [another Mennonite Brethren congregation nearby].

Her husband, LeRoy, added, "We are wondering whether the shaping that goes on with adults in the congregation is not as significant as peer relationships."

College Community was begun in 1962 or 1963, our source was not quite sure which year, by a group who called themselves the "concerned" Mennonites. Gary Nachtigall, dean of students at Fresno-Pacific College remembered the group and the new church, but he could not remember all the issues. One, however, he did recall was their desire to "recapture the Anabaptist vision. This is how I got interested in the church," he said, "though I was not yet married and was 'chasing' girls wherever they were. It quickly became the congregation of the college and seminary faculty and other professional people."

Members of Clovis freely agreed that having so many professors has its limitations. "It creates an ethos for conversation and argument," said Al Dueck, a professor of psychology who had joined the congregation a month before, "but has a danger of becoming just 'talk.' "

Alan Peters agreed. A social worker specializing in child abuse, he said, "We have a body of people on campus thinking about how life should be. Then we have people like me out with the dregs of society saying that it doesn't work. That creates problems—good problems, but not easy ones."

Another characteristic is similarity in age. It is "pretty much a single generation," said Paul Toews, professor of history. We have four or five couples at the most who are beyond 60. We don't have grandparents or grandchildren. There has never been an older generation to temper [us], so I worry about our capacity to bring in the younger."

As if to document his point, a few hours earlier Richard Wiebe, under 30, had told us, "I have seen them move toward traditional practices. The focus has shifted toward the family and the family unit. The sermon topics and orientation are in this direction rather than toward the greater freedom of adults wrestling with their tradition. The service is too focused internally on the needs of the congregation. I would like to see a greater affirmation of the wider church tradition. I see a real divergence between the image of the congregation and the reality."

LeRoy Friesen, minister of the Word (in almost any other congregation he would be called pastor) acknowledged this dilemma. "I think Clovis is a confirmation of what happens to revolutionaries when they win and take over the country. I say that affectionately and in a positive way, but I think that time takes it toll. We are 17 years old and we have our own history—our own ruts—as did the congregations from which we came. That's part of living in history."

Leadership is dispersed at Clovis as one might expect in a congregation running over with talent. Our visit was organized by Bob Enns, moderator of the congregation. His work, as he described it, was more than symbolic. "I am administrative coordinator and chair the church council. LeRoy Friesen and I share the leadership. In addition (1) the council decides the theme of the worship service, (2) the worship commission 'packages' and prepares the bulletin, and (3) the announcement sheet is prepared by LeRoy and me. I meet with him at least twice a week."

After twelve years with Werner Kroeker, its first pastor, the Clovis congregation went for five years without a designated, supported minister. "We decided to try a lay team ministry—unique for Mennonite Brethren—" said Wilfred Martens. "We attempted to discern ministries in the church and have those persons lead us. It was a very tough time and we got exhausted from it. Though our present pastor is leaving we are not likely to go back to lay leadership because of the effort it takes."

LeRoy Friesen, who was leaving after four years, had been a Mennonite Central Committee worker in Jerusalem before his assignment at his home church, Clovis. He was leaving to serve as director of peace studies at Associated Mennonite Biblical Seminaries in Elkhart, Indiana.

I asked about the reentry experience when returning from Jerusalem. "We found it very hard. I think it's harder here in California because of the standard and pace of living. After three years in graduate school and three with MCC, we didn't know how to pay bills!" He commented further on the "tension between the call to discipleship in the use of material goods on the one hand and on the other living in an affluent society in a very prosperous area. We have been

Ruth Enns, plumber, remodeler, and chairman of the Clovis stewardship commission: "I think we are good in crisis situations; sometimes
we think we should invent a crisis to get attention."

people who did not 'sit on our hands' and there is tension about how all of this fits together. We as MB's flirt rather dangerously with the idea that wealth is a blessing of God. One cannot afford to get wealthy uncritically. We have sometimes done this, other times not."

One reason for relative affluence at Clovis is the preponderance of two-income professional families. We have virtually no 'blue collar' workers in the congregation," said Bob Enns, and "virtually no single-income families." Some also were said to do well in development and investments and it was reported that there are millionaires in the congregation.

But the affluence is not reflected in the giving, complained Ruth Enns, chairman of the stewardship commission. "There has been a philosophy that nobody knows how much individuals give. I think we are more secretive about our stewardship than about our sex life. If everyone were giving 2 percent to the budget, we would meet it."

Many in the congregation, it appears, view their occupations as ministry. As Bill Dyck, a dentist, put it, "We do not present ourselves as an 'outreach' church, for we are in outreach through the week."

"A lot of people in the congregation touch a lot of other people during the week," said LeRoy Friesen. "Part of the importance of the congregation is that these come together and instruct and encourage one another. We are sometimes hard on ourselves for not being more in ministry as a corporate body, but I believe in being disciples in the areas of business and professions. I think our main impact is in this."

Yet not all are satisfied to work during the week and attend church on Sunday. They seek a more intense fellowship with one another, some response to the pressures of the economic system, some corporate witness to the world. A

number of these live near each other on Kerckhoff Street in
Fresno and are known by some as the Kerckhoff Street
clique. They meet together for potlucks, assist each other,
and share swimming pools, cars, and tools, especially Bob
Friesen's tools. "Bob Friesen has about every tool you can
think of," said Ruth Enns. Also a California hot tub which is
reportedly good for his back and which the neighbors are
welcome to use.

Another group activity which Bob Friesen mentioned is a
"buying group of 30 families. We get our food from a
warehouse in San Francisco." This is an alternative to stores
like Safeway, which, Bob told us, is an oppressive production
and marketing organization.

Anne Dueck mentioned several couples in the Kerckhoff
area "who are committing themselves to each other in terms
of child rearing and family finances. Some are not paying
war taxes." Another expression of concern was a "Holy
Week Vigil" announced in the congregational newsletter
The M. Bee. This was to be a "daily noon-hour silent vigil at
Fresno's Federal building. The witness offers a 'No' to the
increasing acceptance of militarism and military options by
American society."

Though there is no flag in the Clovis building, not all are
ready to go as far as a vigil and it was reported that such
activity made some members of the congregation very
uneasy. Yet Bill Dyck remarked, "With all the 'personalities'
that exist in the church, I think Clovis is the most cohesive
church in town."

Some persons wondered how we happened to select
Clovis as a congregation to visit out of all the Mennonite
Brethren congregations in the area. I mentioned my friend,
Wally Kroeker, editor of the publication, *The Christian
Leader*, who had given me this name. Al Dueck responded,

"Wally recommended this church with the knowledge that it is a microcosm—from a strong emphasis on pietism and evangelism to an emphasis on social action. Yet there are persons with whom I disagree strongly but our friendship is not broken. There are some morning prayer breakfasts in which there is a good mix of realtors and academic types."

I asked a group of the Kerckhoff people what is important about the church. "The Sunday morning worship service," said Carol Friesen, "and the fellowship."

Her husband, LeRoy, added later, "I think that from the beginning fellowship was seen as especially important. Our son Todd was born ten months after the organization of the congregation and later I had a back operation. Both times the congregation picked us up and carried us along."

Ruth Enns added, "I think we are good in crisis situations, and sometimes we think we should invent a crisis to get attention."

Having heard a great deal about the congregation, we were eager to attend a Sunday morning meeting. Though the service was carefully orchestrated, there was an air of informality that helped to make a visitor comfortable. Elizabeth Kraybill had described it as "a middle ground between structure and informality. There is a choir and you know what to expect, but also you can wear blue jeans if you want to." Some did wear the latest styles, but the minister of the Word ministered in rust-colored corduroy with his collar open. The auditorium is round, seating is on metal chairs, and those who led in worship were close to those being led. Persons in front of the room could see the expression on the face of the choir director.

It was the second Sunday in Lent and the choir sang "Behold the Lamb of God" from Handel's *Messiah* while the minister spoke on "Christ's Passion and Our Loneliness" with a text from Mark 15. "The cup would not pass," he said. "The Father was not going to save Him in the end. The Father was absent. I have no metaphysical explanation for what happened there. But what is clear is that a Jew who believed that God rewarded the righteous was hanging on the cross and was about to die. There would be no escape. The Father was silent and He was totally alone.

"You may ask, 'Where is the good news in all this?' The good news is that because Jesus was alone, you and I never need be alone. And the miracle is that out of this utter isolation comes the formation of a community. A people in whom God's presence is experienced."

After the sermon came the fellowship hour. Adults gathered around a coffee urn on the lawn to welcome visitors and to talk of many things. Less than a majority returned at the ringing of the bell for the adult study hour to hear Les Mark from the seminary tell of ministries to Spanish-speaking people. Even fewer came to an evening meeting to hear representatives of the seminary tell about their aspirations. As a formal meeting, the Sunday morning worship is "it" for the College Community Church.

Before leaving the church we were able to ask Karen Enns, a college-age daughter of Bob and Ruth, about her perception of the congregation. Is this church open to young people?

"I feel comfortable here. When I was younger, there was a problem with Sunday school. We would get a teacher and then the teacher would become tired of the class and we would feel a little rejected. But now I feel at home."

We went to dinner with Delbert and Marjorie Wiens, he a teacher at Fresno Pacific College, she a cardiologist. We talked about the Clovis congregation and its worship services.

Delbert observed the tendency of the congregation to

have ministers who are interested in the tradition of the spiritual quest. "I think the reason why many academics come to Clovis is because theology as a route to holiness is not as impressive to them as it may be to others. This shows itself in poetry and also in the attempt to find esthetic expression.

"For many of us in our rural past, the life of action became a search for God. Then when we discovered systematic theology, we saw it not only as true, but as a way to the mystery of the Godhead. But for those whose job is theology, it becomes secular, so one reaches for the meditative and the esthetic." I had never considered that possibility before.

We talked about a recent effort of the Clovis Mennonite Church, an attempt to draft a covenant for all members of the congregation. It was discussed in the "parishes," a recent grouping of five geographical areas into which all members were placed. The covenant was rejected.

"I don't know what's behind some of the sentiment against it," said Marjorie, "except that some feel there is nothing the church can say to me that would be helpful. I wanted to say to them, 'Why are you in this church?' To me it was not a very constricting thing, but the fact that we heard such negativity made us take another look at it. What it came down to was that most of our parish group could accept the 'I believe' sections, but not the 'practice' sections."

Delbert observed, "My argument was that when each person commits himself to each aspect of what the church is called to do, we are denying the concept of gifts. If every member of the church has to covenant for every aspect of the church's work we end up with a lowest common denominator. On the one hand it demands too much to be committed to all aspects of the work. On the other hand, it demands too little from me."

I received a copy of the proposed covenant from Bob
Enns. Indeed it seemed a far-reaching manuscript, the kind
of wording one would expect from a committee of
professors. It had first an introduction, then an affirmation
and finally a six-section covenant. Each of the six sections included a paragraph which began "I believe" followed by
one beginning "I commit myself." Knowing how hard it is
to draft such statements I could only have regard for those
who had tried and wonder what could be wrong with pledg-
ing, for example, "to recognize the redemptive authority
that Christ has granted to our community and to submit
myself to it; to identify brokenness and sin in our fellowship,
to pray for forgiveness of sin and serve to mediate God's
healing power to my brothers and sisters in Christ; to care
for the integrity of persons who are in need of God's love; to
participate in the discernment sessions where we seek to de-
termine the direction of our life together through the selection of persons and the planning of programs; to serve our
local congregation in the capacity to which it may call me."
On second thought, perhaps some would hesitate to sign
such a statement. I think they would be promising to attend
business meetings, among other things. And this would only
be one of six different commitments!

In an interview with Bob and Ruth Enns, they had spoken
of five issues currently at large in the congregation. First
mentioned was a building program. A bulletin announcement mentioned a groundbreaking the following Sunday for
the next phase of the building program. Not all were convinced it was needed. Indeed Ruth herself had commented
earlier, "We have a circular building with chairs and I see no
reason why we can't bring in tables for our fellowship meals.
I think it's a shame the way a sanctuary is used only three
hours a week. I think a lot of people want to see the church

building improved to keep up with our houses."

A second issue was small groups. "We struggled for years to find a way of organizing small groups. We are individualistic and cliquish. It is hard to find a basis to organize for fellowship." A third issue they mentioned was the covenant discussed above. "Some of the parishioners were very excited about the covenant, some were divided, isolated individuals vociferously opposed it. We finally laid it aside. But it is still an open issue. It was clear that we were going to 'mess with' each other's lives."

A fourth issue was leadership. "Are we going to call a new pastor? The council will start working on this next Monday." A final issue mentioned was "family problems, difficulty in male/female relations. These are extremely explosive."

So we left the Clovis Mennonite Church fascinated by its attempt to bring together diverse and individualistic people and in some sense to disciple them for Jesus.

It was strongly urged that we should not leave Fresno without a visit to the mother community of Reedley, California, 25 miles away. Here Bob and Ruth had grown up and met in Immanuel High School, though he was Mennonite Brethren and she from the General Conference Mennonite Church. Bob's parents took us on a tour of Reedley and Dinuba and explained some of the finer points of fruit growing in this plum, peach, nectarine, almond and grape growing area. It was fruit blossom time and with a little imagination we could have been led to believe that the Garden of Eden was in the San Joaquin Valley and the forbidden fruit a plum.

They took us to visit Reedley Mennonite Brethren Church, the largest Mennonite congregation in North America. There are nearly 1,400 in the congregation and the auditorium seats 1,850. In addition, there is a chapel seating some 300, for smaller funerals, weddings, and similar activities.

We were awed by the building, the size of the staff, and the calendar. It is a style of doing church with which we are not familiar. Ed Toews, minister of Christian education and evangelism, showed us his map of the area with a pin for each family unit. He explained that there are 30 to 35 deacon couples and each couple is expected to be responsible for the nurture of a group within the congregation. So they have recognized that even with a pastor, associate pastor, and associate ministers of Christian education, music and youth, the staff cannot relate directly to 1,400 people. Indeed it was acknowledged that there are in effect distinct separate congregations in the morning service based on where they sit and which doors they leave by. The ministers circulate from door to door in order to shake hands with different people. And Pastor H. H. Dick has called for the wearing of name tags.

It occurred to me that Reedley Mennonite Brethren Church is rather like a district conference of 1,400 members with some 30 separate small congregations as indicated by the 30 deacon couples. They meet together on Sunday mornings in their large auditorium, then go their separate ways.

One advantage they have which is lacking at Clovis is the staff and the members to organize a full-blown youth program. They also were planning a passion play on "3 Big Nights," April 4, 5, and 6. Music Minister Bob Plett was working on the cast for the play. Another notable item on the calendar: "Our 75th year celebration, weekend of June 14, 15."

John Enns spoke briefly about his family's coming to Reedley. "My grandparents came in 1904; my parents in

1905. They came from Kansas." Why did they come? Reedley was a secondary settlement. His grandfather had come to the United States about ten years after the main push of Russian Mennonites into the United States. Probably the better lands were already taken in Kansas. Also, the San Joaquin Valley climate resembles southern Russia from whence they had come.

Fruit farming is an intensive form of agriculture. I asked John how many acres of the land a farmer needs to make a living. "Forty to 80 acres are probably considered enough to make a living," he said. But there is trouble. The farmland is selling for eight to ten thousand dollars an acre and in John's opinion that is a greater investment than one can expect to carry by fruit farming. So there is no Eden without its dark side.

The radicals at Clovis are growing older and there is lack of grandparents in the church. Some of them are 25 miles away at Reedley. Others are thousands of miles away at Winnipeg, Manitoba. But a few are nearer at hand, and the Bob Friesens have found a way out of their dilemma. "I think it's good for a group to have grandparents," said Bob. "For our family, my parents live close to Clovis and we have breakfast with them every Sunday morning."

11
A Mennonite Presence in Haight-Ashbury

I first heard of Haight-Ashbury during the hippie era in the sixties. To this section of San Francisco came the flower children to smoke their pot and dream their dreams of a world without violence—and work. The flower children are gone now, at least Mary and I did not recognize any on our weekend visit to that area. But we did meet a representative group of the 9-member Haight-Ashbury Mennonite Fellowship, a name that had taken them three hours to decide upon less than a week before.

We found the fellowship at a crucial time, though from what they told us cruciality had been characteristic of their experience during the five years of their life. Known as the San Francisco Mennonite Fellowship until the name change mentioned above, the group had roots going back to 1975 with leadership by James and Leanna Rhodes. It had served as a rallying place for scattered Mennonites, an opportunity for a small corporate presence and witness, and a base for Voluntary Service.

Dan Ponthieux said he was glad to see the fellowship begin. "I was the first Mennonite in the city," said Dan.

(How he determined this I do not know, but I have no statistics to refute it.) "There were no Mennonite churches here and after ten years I was thinking of going back to the East. Then I met James and Leanna Rhodes," and as he expressed his sentiments in a meeting of the fellowship, "it gives me great pleasure to be here today."

James and Leanna Rhodes were no longer in the city. They had left about six months before we came somewhat disillusioned with the possibilities of building a church and raising a family in the city. So for the history of the fellowship, we were referred to Stephana Roth who first came to San Francisco for Voluntary Service in January 1977. Stephana remembered that there had been two fellowships at that time. "One met on Sunday morning and sang out of *The Mennonite Hymnal.* Another met in evenings, a hang-loose type. The morning group was comprised of persons with a Mennonite background." At about the time Stephana arrived in San Francisco the two groups merged.

In March 1980, three years after the merger, there had been a complete turnover in leadership and there was now a new name. Copastor Ken Reed gave two reasons for the name change. For one, there were plans to begin a Mennonite witness to Vietnamese people in San Francisco sponsored by the General Conference Mennonite Church and led by Fred King. San Francisco Fellowship had no interest in being known as "First Mennonite." A second reason was to identify with their neighborhood, to give a sign that they were seeking to minister in Haight-Ashbury.

The second concern was augmented by their new meetinghouse, a two-room basement facility just rented. Mary and I performed a small voluntary service assignment: we helped to paint the new Haight-Ashbury Mennonite meetinghouse. They looked forward to the meetinghouse. Cur-

Stephana Roth of Haight-Ashbury Mennonite Fellowship helping to prepare the new meeting place.

rently they were meeting in the living room of the Voluntary Service house where 15 people could sit in a comfortable circle. The meetinghouse would make room for growth.

The Haight-Ashbury Fellowship included basically three types of persons: (1) Mennonites who had come to the city for other reasons, but were glad to have a fellowship there; (2) current or former Voluntary Service persons; and (3) seekers for light who have found the fellowship a place to minister and be ministered to.

Ken and Kathy Reed came to San Francisco from eastern Pennsylvania because in Kathy's word they "were feeling a little disillusioned with materialism and wanted to get away."

As Ken put it, "We didn't want to end up at age 50 with a big stone house and two cars." They were interested in Voluntary Service and were attracted to San Francisco because they heard a fellowship was about to begin. As did Stephana Roth, they stayed in San Francisco after their term of service was completed.

They now were the parents of an eight-month-old son, David, whose care they were sharing, each having a part-time job. Ken worked three days as Refugee Airport Coordinator for Church World Service, and Kathy two days in the library of Bridgemont School, a Christian school where she had done her Voluntary Service. They lived without a car, the old Hornet having sustained fatal damage in an accident two months before.

In the fall of 1979, Ken found leadership thrust upon him when James Rhodes left. "I didn't want to be a pastor. When I was a boy others saw me in this role and I reacted against it. But then when I found myself in a leadership role, it was not the stereotyped pastor I had rejected and I was able to accept it."

The schedule of our Sunday with the Reeds was a little different from our usual Sunday pattern. Their Sunday service is held from 5:00 to 7:00 p.m. I wondered why. "When we began, it made it easier to invite people to our meetings; Haight types are more 'lively' in the evening. In addition, persons who go away for the weekend can get back in time for church. We first met at 7:00 p.m., but that was too late. Also, we had a potluck before the service, but it was hard to get from the former to the latter. Now we meet at 5:00 and follow with a potluck every two weeks. In addition, we have a potluck at our Wednesday evening meeting."

So we began that Sunday by sleeping late and eating brunch with the Reeds and Stephana Roth. Then we took a walk to Golden Gate park. It was a pleasant sunny day, but with the cool breeze for which San Francisco is famous. We spent a little time in a museum while David and his mother rested on the grass. Then we had a picnic, visited the Japanese tea garden, and strolled over to the VS center for the evening meeting. The fifteen plus in attendance included four visitors and two children. There was not room for many more. The two-hour meeting had the church as its theme. As Ken Reed proclaimed in his welcome, it was "the first meeting of the Haight-Ashbury Mennonite Fellowship." There was singing from *The Mennonite Hymnal* and from special chorus sheets. Stephana Roth accompanied on her flute. Ken Reed gave a meditation on "What Is the Church?" using H. S. Bender's article in *The Mennonite Encyclopedia* as his source. Then he called for sharing on the question, "What is one good church experience you have had?" Since there were only two children, there was no Sunday school, but Jim Pawling read two stories from *God Keeps His Promise* to his seven-year-old son, Jeffrey, while the whole congregation listened. Then there were reports from the visiting journalists, and finally the potluck. Except for needing to do interviews, it was a day of rest.

I had asked Stephana Roth as congregational "historian" how the fellowship had changed in the three years since it

Jim Pawling reads from *God Keeps His Promise* to his son Jeffrey, the only child in church at Haight-Ashbury Mennonite Fellowship.

began. "We have become more deliberate about planning
our Sunday evening meetings. Also, more deliberate about
leadership and more evangelistic in terms of bringing in
people. For a time we used our Sunday evening meeting for
discussion of our congregational covenant. This was not at-
tractive to visitors, so now we make our Sunday evening
meetings inspirational. But what really brings people in is
our life together, not the program. We have always tried to
be a witness to our neighbors, but having a better formed
leadership has helped us, and a more deliberate planning."

Mobility is a fact of life for a small fellowship such as
Haight-Ashbury. People move in. People move out. Some
may do it more than once. Mobility is a characteristic of
urban life and thus affects all urban churches, but it is felt
most strongly by a young, small fellowship. "Having
transients means that each year you have to explain everything again. Mennonite community doesn't just happen
here. You have to sit down and have hours and hours of
meetings," said Ken.

In an effort to develop a committed core and a beginning
toward stability, the fellowship developed three categories of
membership. As Ken described them these were: (1) full
members, the persons making the major decisions; (2)
associate members, free to come and go; (3) co-pilgrims,
persons "who are with us in spirit, but cannot be present all
the time. Although we made these categories with good
intentions, they cause problems. We need to wrestle with
what it means to be a member."

Jim Pawling had not been in Voluntary Service nor was he
a Mennonite when he came to the area. "What attracted
you to this fellowship?" I asked him. "An exposure through
literature to Anabaptist principles. Initially it was Jim Wallis'
Agenda for Biblical People recommended to me on

August 7, 1978, by the Bartimaeus Missionary Society which showed a film called *Brother Sun, Sister Moon* (a good film, by the way). After a showing I mentioned I was reading Wallis' book. They replied, 'This is one of our textbooks.' So I got their reading list.

"Wallis' book provided me a rational imperative and left me with a great hunger for a different way of life. Then I got Dave and Neta Jackson's *Living Together in a World Falling Apart.* In the bibliography I found books of the Society of Brothers and sent away for some of these. I also read *Rich Christians in an Age of Hunger* by Ronald Sider. After considerable reading I went back and said, 'The church I am in is not going this way,' and I was referred to the Mennonite fellowship. So I signed in as an associate member in March or April 1979 when their covenant was firmed up. This was a couple of months after I had visited the Society of Brothers at Farmington, Pennsylvania. I concluded that whatever part of the vision I cannot work out 'in community' I want to work at here as far as I can."

Jim was formerly a member of the Jehovah's Witnesses and his wife continued in that group. "For me belonging to this fellowship means coming to San Francisco seven days a week. I'm fragmented. I feel conflicts between job, church, and family." Jim's best dream would be to regain spiritual unity with his wife and for them together to go into an intentional community. But he considers it a ministry of Haight-Ashbury "to have something to say to people whose situations are less than ideal."

Some in the fellowship at one time were an intensive community. As Ken Reed recalled, they "shared incomes and expenses. We were all 'keen' on the idea but it raised a number of problems. People who were members of the fellowship but not of the community felt they were getting left out of important decisions. Before we knew it we would get into matters that affected the whole group. Also we spent a lot of 'heavy' sessions talking about small matters."

What stopped it?

"We had a 'little Watergate.' We had always said that those who did not have employment could do volunteer service while looking for work. But it developed that those who earned the most money felt that those who were unemployed or making less were spending 'their' money. So we dissolved the intentional community." It was rumored that there was some interest in beginning again, but we heard no clear word on this.

Lois Janzen came to Haight-Ashbury by still another route. She graduated from Goshen Biblical Seminary in the spring of 1979. With a background in teaching and training for pastoral work, she considered what she might do and vacillated between the one and the other. "I had had 'team ministry' experience in several churches and rather liked it. But the openings I found were for Christian education directors and I was not interested in a Christian education position. People began suggesting to me that I look for a small group where I could teach for my living and work my way into pastoring. Mennonite Board of Missions gave me names of some cities where there were small fellowships and I wrote to San Francisco. From them I learned of Bridgemont, a Christian High School, and was able to get a job as a teacher."

"I wouldn't have come to San Francisco without the job at Bridgemont, but my fears about teaching proved true. I was not on the same wavelength as teenagers. Though I liked the school, I did not like the paper work involved with the teaching. But I had a good feeling about my work with the church. After Christmas Bridgemont allowed me to break my contract.

"In October the fellowship had clearly decided not to license me to the ministry, but the week after my release at Bridgemont Stanley Weaver (Southwest Mennonite Conference overseer based in Phoenix, Arizona) came and we talked about the Scriptures and the ministry of women. At the end of the day the fellowship asked for me to be licensed. I have not yet signed the license application, but I expect to do so."

What strengths do you have to offer in the pastoral ministry?

"One is concern for the individual; I do not have a strong corporate sense. I think I can bring to the group an unwillingness to fear being small and to fear singleness. I like the diversity of an urban church where unity doesn't mean sameness. I think it is important to find some way of being a place of celebration and rest from all the other things that happen otherwise—one place where the barriers that normally exist in the city are broken down."

I asked Ken Reed how he and Lois divided the pastoral responsibility. "Before we began," he replied, "we thought my gift would be contacts with the broader church and administration, and Lois would do the traditional pastoral things: Bible study and counseling. But we both do counseling and I am doing a series of Bible studies. I think our relationship is still being defined because we have somewhat different ideas of how the church might develop. We have different backgrounds—she has had pastoral experience and has been to a Mennonite seminary—but I often sound more traditional than she.

"As with so many things in our fellowship, we did not sit down and plan this—it just happened. I think there is a strength here. We did not have a theory first, just experience, and on the basis of our experience, we organized."

Another form of organization Ken mentioned which just happened was the mission groups. "We started mission groups because we had to find out what we were called to do. The first mission group got started because not everyone felt called to or comfortable with a protest at the Lockheed plant. So at a November meeting, we had people say what they would like to be involved in and ended up with three: (1) the peace mission group, (2) yeast ministries (friendship evangelism), and (3) Bridgemont High School. (This has been our most significant Voluntary Service involvement, but we had not been saying anything to the school.)"

Among the activities of the peace mission group was preparing a mailing for all the pastors in San Francisco which would include two tracts raising issues related to the biblical imperative toward peace. Also they prepared a proposal to the Schowalter Foundation seeking funds to establish a peace library.

Not that emphasis on peace is lacking in San Francisco. "There is a strong pacifist movement in the Bay area," said Ken, "but it is not Christian. We go to demonstrations and pass out literature. People are surprised that a church is interested in peacemaking and wonder 'what are you doing here with the atheists?' "

Jim Pawling stressed the importance of showing "that a church as church is putting Christ up front at the same time it is taking peace seriously." He observed that the demonstration at Lockheed "showed us that doing things with coalition groups can compromise the message." He reported also that "we are asking questions about what elements of peace ministry there are beside opposition to war—neighborhood peace, promoting reconciliation between criminal and victim. This has been our growing edge."

Since present Voluntary Service workers were a significant bloc in the fellowship, I chatted with several of them and asked about the contribution of the fellowship to their experience. Sherry Maddox replied that it was the other way around. "The fellowship depends on us. We make up one third of the group. When they are looking over VS applications, they pick those who seem to be stable in order that they may contribute to the life of the fellowship."

But the VS group seemed not unhappy with San Francisco, and, as others have done, considered remaining in the city after their service period was over. Steve Nice commented that "we all have decided that we would not stay on in Voluntary Service, but would remain in the city. After being involved in a city of 650,000 people with an emerging group, I would feel guilty going back home."

Later I asked Ken Reed whether having a unit was considered a part of the church program. He replied that "Voluntary Service (as sponsored by Mennonite Board of Missions in Elkhart, Indiana) sees their work as helping churches get started. Last September we had a VS evaluation. Bob Hovde (regional director) was here. Rick Stiffney (director of Relief and Service) was here. They concluded that since the Rhodes' were leaving they weren't sure the fellowship would make it and they talked of pulling out the unit also. They threatened a bit—'if you don't get your act together.' So that made us scramble. But now there is a new mood. Recently Bob Hovde was here and wondered when they could send in four more persons.

"One of the good things about a VS unit is that it keeps our fingers in various community activities such as Bridgemont High School and the Alcoholic Center where Steve Nice works. There is a word of caution though—if this is how we grow we could end up as a transplant Mennonite community.

"Right now we have a handful of applications to work through. Anybody who comes here is expected to be interested in planting a church and mature enough to handle the city environment. The San Francisco VS unit has gotten the reputation of being a tough place to get into. We haven't had to spend a lot of time 'holding hands.' "

And what of the future at the Haight-Ashbury Mennonite Fellowship? Stephana Roth observed that "you will always have transients. I hope we can reach some people who want to live in San Francisco and become a real peace witness community."

Dana Brown, a student at San Francisco Theological Seminary, had chosen to observe Haight-Ashbury as an assignment for a class at the seminary. On the Sunday evening of our visit, she interviewed Ken Reed. One of the questions she asked was, "What is your strategy?"

Ken later reported his reaction to the question. "Strategy? To survive as a fellowship! We don't have enough time for reflection. We just proceed from crisis to crisis. Our strategy is to maintain an Anabaptist-Mennonite presence in San Francisco!"

Haight-Ashbury was the youngest congregation yet visited on this trip. Germantown was the oldest. It occurred to me that in their present forms, these two fellowships at opposite ends of the continent had a number of things in common. Both are small, operate without a supported ministry, yet are seeking to cherish the Anabaptist heritage and spread the news of God's love. Both appear frail in the light of what they are up against. But both will continue and grow if they have vision, courage, and energy such as they currently show.

12
A Sense of Something Beginning to Happen

It is hard to find anything unusual about the Albany (Ore.) Mennonite Church. At 80 years, it is not old for a congregation. At some 200 members, it is neither large nor small. It has a 1950s Mennonite building set in an open area. Membership median is neither very young nor very old, though there are sixteen widows. It is by its own admission not particularly successful in evangelism. It is on the surface just an average Mennonite church where people care for one another in the same manner as we had come to expect from our earlier contacts on the trip.

But there were some local variations on the theme and certain intensities. For example, in contact after contact I heard people troubled about the problems of the divorced and remarried and wondering how the congregation could be helpful to them because there was not a common mind on how to deal with this issue. Evidently one reason for this concern was a high divorce rate in the city of Albany. According to church secretary Faye Claassen it is one in three.

"A lady where I work is looking for a church home," said Faye. "I think we have what she needs. But her husband is her second husband and I hesitate to invite her. If you are going to be helpful to people, you have to face these things. I wish we would know. I wish there were something very clear."

Clysta Buerge, one of the elders, acknowledged the lack of unanimity in the church. "We have had occasion at least to attempt to come to grips with the issue, but we have strong opinions. We will need to absorb counsel, get more insight. It's an ongoing subject."

The marital problems have not all been outside the congregation as some reported frankly. "This congregation didn't mean much to me until Cheryl and I were separated for three months," said Glen Landis. "Coming back to Cheryl I found the church was important and I have opened myself to others in the church."

His wife, Cheryl, agreed. "A number of people were a support to me. The hardest thing for me to do was to go to church. But I took the risk and I got the support. Now I know that the support is there, I feel really good about the church because there have been some really hard things in people's lives. As these are shared in prayer, it is really neat."

Glen and Cheryl were in a group of three young married couples talking about their relationship to the Albany congregation. They agreed that Pastor James (Jim) Lapp had a key role in their participation. We talked about the young adult church dropout problem.

Darrell Fisher described his experience. He had grown up in the Albany congregation, "went away to college and service and kind of left the church." He married Stephanie, a Catholic girl, "and then came to Albany. We went from church to church and finally to Albany Mennonite." One experience that encouraged them was "the time Jim came and talked to Steph and me when we were showing up

Jim Lapp (right) pastor at Albany: "I have tried to affirm the gifts of members and to share the spiritual oversight with the elders."

about once a month. He wondered what the church could
do for us and suggested that ours was a searching age and he
accepted this."

In fact, members of various age-groups spoke well of Jim
Lapp, a person-oriented pastor who held four-year-old Katie
Friesen on his lap during a Sunday evening meeting. He
had come to Albany from eastern Pennsylvania in 1972.
Mabel Schlegel, a retired widow, said of him, "When he is
in a group every person seems to matter to him."

Verna Birky, who recently moved back to Oregon from
Indiana, said, "Jim is just tops."

Church council chairman Amos Conrad said, "Things go
well with Jim Lapp. He's a dynamic person but also easy to
work with. He tells it like it is. I like that. If I do something
he doesn't like, he tells me."

Praise for the pastor was not completely uniform. There
were a few critics who spoke of his "perfectionism" and implied that even when he urged others to help with the work
of the church, he tended to control the manner of their participation. But even here there was confidence in him, for
one of the critics said, "If I were ever in deep tragedy, there
is no one I would rather have next to me than Jim Lapp."

We talked to Jim about his role in the congregation. He
acknowledged that "more than I wish, the church centers
around me." But he told of his efforts to de-clericalize.
"Back in Pennsylvania I was only a half-time pastor and
people did not call me 'pastor.' Here there was a tendency to
put me on a pedestal. When I came the pulpit was on the
highest level. I soon moved it down lower to be closer to the
people." (Evidently Jim had been successful in one part of
his campaign. During the three days we spent at Albany, we
did not hear one person call him "Pastor"!)

Jim indicated his perception of his own role as an "enabling ministry." He reported that the church had a new constitution when he arrived and implied it was not all he desired. "I and they had to learn to live with it. In theory and theology I have tried to affirm the gifts of members and to share the spiritual oversight with the elders. I do most of the preaching and a lot of teaching, mostly elective Sunday school classes."

Some reported they were being weaned from overdependence on the pastor. "We used to say that we were at the church because of Jim," said Nancy Friesen, "but now I think relationships are developing so that we can make it if he leaves."

Her husband, Jerry, admitted, "I waited for some years to change my membership because I wasn't sure I could survive without him."

The organization of the congregation appeared somewhat complex. There are the elders, the church council, and four commissions: (1) worship and nurture, (2) stewardship and resources, (3) witness and service, and (4) fellowship and caring. "I have regularly tried to meet with the chairpersons of these commissions, and tried to help them think through their leadership and consider issues. I try to communicate that the church does not belong to me. My function is to provide support."

Lester Kropf, chairman of the elders, acknowledged the new insight regarding congregational leadership. "We have gone from a plural ministry to a salaried pastor and now there is a trend back toward involving more people. I think Albany was the first in our district to have a salaried pastor. Now we are asking whether this was the best. Actually, we have gone full circle."

Most people we talked to spoke with appreciation for the congregation. Lloyd Zehr said, "A real caring group. If you have a need, everyone pitches in." His wife, Fern, agreed. "It has always felt good. I've often wondered why we always like Albany Mennonite Church so well."

Mabel Schlegel said, "I have a good feeling. Our pastor is a compassionate person and some of the young people can be quite close too."

Joan Kropf, a young adult, said, "The majority of the leadership comes from an older age-group, but I do feel there is an opportunity for younger ones to function. I am chairman of the worship and nurture commission. Others younger than I are also involved." But Joan sometimes feels that "if I were older and male, my requests for people to do things might carry more weight."

Marilyn Holderread, another young adult, said of the congregation, "Sometimes I really feel a part of it and sometimes I don't." Yet she said, "I feel a community there. There are people to whom I can relate."

In general it seemed that married persons felt more at home. Lois Kenagy said, "I really look forward to Sunday morning."

Larry and Cathy Passmore agreed. Larry said, "When I bring someone to church I am confident that there will be a string of people coming to meet them because they really want to know who these visitors are. I know there will be a fantastic sermon and good music. This is in contrast to my former church which could have used the same bulletin for the last 20 years. Nothing ever changed."

Some also observed that the degree of belonging was affected by the degree of involvement. Stephanie Fisher said, "I think a lot of our growth in the church has been our willingness to be a part of it."

Nancy Friesen added, "The more involved you get, the more you put in and the more you want to put in. It seems there are those who just sit there and dust the pews. It's judgmental, but I want to say, 'Get involved!' ''

The self-appointed critic of the Albany congregation was Joe Wannemacher, a regular participant but not a member. "I visited every other church in the area including Mormons." Then someone told him about Albany Mennonite and he came. "I feel a little frustrated because there is a lot of good will in the church, but not enough good methods of learning how to live a Christian life. I like the church. I'm stuck with it, but somehow it's not as productive as it could be. From the production point of view its goals are too vague. People are too much attached to fixed points like tithing. Christ said, 'If you have two, give one away.' We should take Christ as the ideal and see what we can do. I think the congregation does not expect enough from each member."

In an effort to put more muscle into membership requirements, Albany considered a covenant, a feature we had observed in some younger congregations. Elder Howard Claassen remembered that it "was discussed at business meeting but it was difficult to get agreement on a statement that people would sign. Some of the things that have happened in their background made them fear that we are trying to make people conform rather than respond voluntarily."

I mentioned the covenant to the age thirty group and some had difficulty remembering it. But Nancy Friesen said, "It was acceptable to me. It did not make me feel pressured and was in line with my beliefs. It also became an occasion for conversation with another person about my Christian life and I thought it was a good thing."

A revised form of the covenant appeared on a leaflet called "Introducing the Albany Mennonite Church." It included a brief history of the congregation, a covenant of

membership, and a 10-point list of general membership expectations that concluded with "10. That each member
practice a daily lifestyle in keeping with the teachings and
example of Jesus." What could be more reasonable than
this?

A concern of some at Albany was limited success in evangelism. But they took some satisfaction in having helped to
found Mennonite churches at Logsden, Corvallis, Salem,
and Lebanon. "There were other congregations involved
also," as Lester Kropf acknowledged, "but Albany supplied
sizable numbers. It was a good feeling that this could happen, though we missed them when they left."

It was also pointed out that Albany has had a good record
of people going into Voluntary Service and Mennonite
Central Committee work. They told about Adella Gingerich
who has four children. At one time three of them were in
service and she herself was helping at the International
Guest House, Washington, D.C. Also Jim Lapp had just
completed a term as moderator of Pacific Coast district
conference, and Lois Kenagy served as chairman of their
peace and social concerns committee as well as being a
member of the Mennonite Board of Education. John Shantz
was on a special Mennonite Central Committee West Coast
Task Force related to developmental disabilities.

Leaders at Albany had scheduled a Methodist Lay Wit-
ness mission to be held in the congregation. Jim Lapp said,
"I am hoping this may be one step toward sharing our faith.
I am sure our congregation has a witness beyond ourselves."

When the present Albany meetinghouse was erected in
the fifties, it was positioned with the hope that housing
would be developed around it. But then land in the vicinity
was zoned for industrial development and traffic on
Interstate 5 rushed past nearby. So although there are many

dwellings not far away, it has not become the residential community they expected.

Like most of the formerly rural churches we visited, many at Albany can remember when the population was much smaller and life simpler than it is today. The sign at the edge of Albany said "population 28,000." Mabel Schlegel could remember when it was 5,000. Albert Steckley, a farmer who had lived with one wife for 63 years, looked toward the city from Mabel's living room and said, "We used to thresh over toward the center of Albany."

Mabel Schlegel, longtime resident of Albany who can remember when the town was less than one fifth its size: "It used to be you knew everybody." Farmer Albert Steckley of Albany Mennonite Church: "We used to thresh over toward the center of Albany."

And Anna Kennel told how her husband, John, looked at a housing development and said, "I used to bale that field."

Mabel said, "It used to be you knew everybody. You went downtown and could recognize everyone. Today it's different and when you are older, you notice it. This winter, I began to have 'nuisance' telephone calls."

Some of the industries which moved into the expanded Albany are quite specialized. According to Lester Kropf, Albany is the rare metals capital of the world, producing metals such as zirconium used in nuclear reactors.

Cathy Passmore with Joe Wannemacher, resident critic of the Albany congregation. Albany members had near uniform praise for their congregation, but Joe demurred. "I like the church," said Joe. "I'm stuck with it. But it could be more productive."

Clysta Buerge added, "We have Oregon Freeze Dry from which food products went to the moon."

Some of the industrial activity "created a lot of smoke and smells" in the words of Jerry Brenneman. Also Albany "is still the center of a lot of lumber industries. They are trying to promote the kind of industry that is more compatible with the population."

These changes in employment are reflected in the Albany congregation. As Viola Kropf observed, "There are half a dozen farmers, but also teachers, professional people. The makeup of our congregation as far as employment is much different than it used to be." Among the farmers is congregational chairman Amos Conrad who farms 1,500 acres and raises grain, grass seed, and sheep. Grass seed and sheep culture go well together as the sheep can be pastured on the grass which is later allowed to mature for seed. We learned that the going rate for sheep pasturing was 3¢ per head per day.

Another effect of the growth in the Albany population has been that high school students from the congregation are located in three different school districts in addition to the conference-sponsored Western Mennonite School at Salem. As a consequence of this scattering the young people have conflicting schedules and little desire to be together in a congregational youth program.

"We meet at a variety of times," said Larry Passmore, one of the sponsors. "Some cut out at one time, others at another. The most successful thing lately was a district wide youth activity at Western Mennonite School which ran from 10:00 p.m. until 2:00 a.m."

Dick Myer, the conference youth director, had suggested an emphasis of one-to-one relationships between adults and young people. Kathy Passmore commented that "as a youth sponsor I feel more need to go where they are. When you have a kid in your group who is on a team and you go to see him play, you can't talk to him then, but you can later." She told of having waited more than an hour outside a restaurant for a young man to leave work so that she could talk to him.

It seemed also that other aspects of the Albany congregation's work was done by individuals and small groups rather than in concert.

Faye Claassen observed that "we have several people who do things very quietly. I try to find such people and give them a boost." She noted also, "I think one of the strengths of our congregation is the way the elderly are organized for prayer. At Christmas, Jim suggested that we remember students away at college. So I thought, 'now let's see if they will.' And the one card our daughter Jennelle got came from a quiet person I least expected. It's this kind of caring that is really nice."

Jim Lapp was seeking to encourage the development of gifts within the congregation. "I have been trying to ask who in the church seem to be catching the vision of what I think the church should become and investing time with them. I go to workshops for my own growth and I am also taking lay people along."

He noted also that "in the last year or two some of the significant change in the church has come through crises in members' lives." A number of these were marital crises and these had led to an emphasis on participation in workshops to strengthen marriages. Also "last year my wife, Nancy, had surgery and the congregation ministered to us."

"I feel we are on the frontier of something," he said. "I'm not sure what. I think it ought to lead to people outside hearing the good news and coming into the church. There is a sense of something beginning to happen here."

13
The Church as Family

"For most of us, the church is a substitute family," said Lauren Friesen, pastor of the South Seattle Mennonite Church. I see a lot of celebration done in church that in a traditional Mennonite community would be done in a family gathering." One reason is that 90 percent of the South Seattle Mennonites have come from somewhere else. Indeed many other people in Seattle have come from somewhere else.

They have responded to educational and economic activities in Seattle, Washington, a fast-paced city sprawled between Puget Sound and Lake Washington and draped over several hills and smaller lakes so that it has almost as many traffic traps for the visitor as Pittsburgh, Pennsylvania.

Mennonites are not populous in the state of Washington. There are nine congregations in all. South Seattle is a young congregation, small, and transient. It began bravely in 1968 when the charter group purchased an old supper club as a meetinghouse for $18,000 and called Milton Harder as pastor. The congregation developed as expected until 1972 when a recession hit Seattle. The Boeing Company laid off

130,000 of its 200,000 employees and people of all sorts began to leave the area. South Seattle's numbers were decimated, its morale dropped, and Milton Harder was constrained to seek other employment.

Two years later Lauren Friesen was assigned as pastor and he remembers that 12 people appeared for service on the first Sunday. By early 1980 there were 90 active people with an attendance varying from 45 to 75. A majority of the congregation is young. There were only three couples in the forties, one in the fifties, and one in the seventies. "A lot of the people are still at the age of sorting out life goals, exploring the possibility of changing careers, training for a new area," said Lauren Friesen. The result is a constant turnover in congregational personnel.

According to Mona Elston, "When we first voted for church officers, we had six-month terms because people were not sure they would be here longer."

Lauren said "We once prided ourselves on being the best 'farewell' congregation."

"But it was hard," added his wife, Janet.

And Kay Schrag remarked, "It affected how close you wanted to get to people."

But now they took courage in a little more stability, though they expected that coming and going would continue to be a feature of their church life. As an example, we had lunch with Leon and Marjorie Hershberger, South Seattle participants for the past 3½ years while Leon studied chemistry at the University of Washington. But his study program was coming to an end and within six months Leon was scheduled to take a position in Wilmington, Delaware, within easy driving distance of Leon's and Marjorie's parents, but far from their substitute family in Seattle.

Former congregational chairman Lucy Harms was philosophical about the goings. "It's hard, but then you zero in on how much richer our life is because we have allowed them into our family." But, as she observed, a relatively high student population cuts into congregational support. In a letter to the Pacific District Conference in the spring of 1979, Lucy reported "about 10 stable wage earning units" plus seven graduate students, three medical students, eight college students, nine in Voluntary Service, nine who had finished VS or school within the year, and one retired household." Because of the nature of its membership the congregation requested continued partial subsidy from the conference.

Resident grandparents at South Seattle were Quintus and Miriam Leatherman, former directors of a student center in London, England, under Mennonite Board of Missions. They retired in Seattle because they had a son in the area who supplied them a house—and because they liked the climate. "I had never quite been able to take the heat of summer in eastern Pennsylvania," said Miriam.

I wondered how a congregation of principally younger people would minister to them in their seventies. "Through visitation by Lauren," said Quintus. "Also recently through a small group which meets at least once a month."

Miriam said, "I think the young people are very good. We have been told repeatedly that they are glad to have someone older. We feel highly accepted."

The congregation of South Seattle seemed about as informal as I had yet encountered. The definition of membership also. The main organizational structure, said congregational chairman Jim Eby, is an advisory committee of seven members which functions like a church council. The seven are the chairman, secretary, treasurer, Sunday school coordinator, peace and social concerns director, direc-

Quintus and Miriam Leatherman, resident "grandparents" at South Seattle: "We feel highly accepted."

tor of maintenance and Mennonite Disaster Service, and the pastor.

Matters of concern to the congregation and not provided or in the structure are sometimes carried forward by volunteers. "If people want to do something," said Kay Schrag, "they get together and do it."

As a strategy for fellowship and decision making, the congregation was divided into small groups, assigned on a random basis. "In addition to being a sounding board for the Advisory Committee, small groups can set their own agenda," said Jim Eby. Facilities was the issue before the congregation in March of 1980. The old supper club was getting tight and it was agreed that something should be done.

Options were identified as follows: (1) expand, (2) build, (3) buy an existing facility, (4) rent a building from another Christian group, or (5) share a building with another congregation too small to use its building to the best advantage. A study group had been established to feed questions to the small groups and seek to narrow the options.

A complicating factor was the location of the supper club on the extreme southern edge of the Mennonite residences in Seattle. Most of the present congregation lives farther north, though a few come from as far south as Tacoma. Lucy Harms hoped "that another congregation will grow up in the south—a sister congregation—perhaps one that will share a pastor. How this will happen is frightening, but I guess that is faith."

Membership is defined quite informally at South Seattle. Anyone who attends regularly and participates is allowed to vote. "We have not been strong on creedal or semi-creedal statements," said Lauren Friesen. "We have focused more on relationships than specific beliefs or specific words. At one point a person wanted to join the congregation in order to explore whether Christianity is worthwhile. He appreciated the Mennonite heritage and wanted to experience membership as a way of discovering faith. The church affirmed this and he came in."

There is no congregational statement of faith. "Four years ago a number of people were concerned to have a statement," reported Jim Eby. "So they got together and drafted one, but I don't know where it is."

In spite of such an apparent easygoing attitude on membership and standards, 76-year-old Miriam Leatherman said, "In all my meanderings in the church I have never found a congregation where such a high percentage was so serious about the church."

One of the more serious was Tim Mierau, director of the congregation's peace and social concerns emphasis. He considered it a measure of congregational commitment that the director of this program is included on the advisory committee. In a brief conversation he spoke of some local peace issues: (1) the Trident submarines with the first subs scheduled to arrive in Puget Sound the following summer, (2) registration and a possible draft, (3) a hope that it might be possible to do counter recruiting in schools where the military recruiters operate, (4) war tax resistance. Last year he and his wife had claimed a war crimes credit on their income tax report. This year they were resisting more directly, refusing to pay about $300.

"Naturally I would like to have more congregational interest, but I think we have the most active, or at least sympathetic, congregation I know of," he said. There is no objection to my presentations during the Sunday school hour. When I come with challenges there is generally a favorable response. People are personally supportive."

According to Lauren Friesen, 35 to 40 percent of the congregation has come from a background other than Mennonite. "I don't think at this point there is a conscious distinction between traditional Mennonites and others except when it comes to talking about our families in places like Goshen, Indiana or Newton, Kansas."

How has the church found these people? "Mostly by contacts in school or at work. They were invited to the church and they came." Actually, it was a little more complex than this as we learned when we talked to some of the newer people.

David Bell and Barbara Havlin (husband and wife, but she keeps her former name) came to Seattle from California for David to study at Seattle-Pacific College. They became unhappy with their Assemblies of God and Baptist traditions and set out to find another church tradition. Non-specificity on war, conservative politics, and flag waving were some things that troubled them. Also a legalistic, literalistic view of the Bible and a failure to allow women to really "work" in the church except in the kitchen. "We couldn't agree with any tradition that would have an oppressive view of God," said Dave.

So they went to the library to study church traditions and found themselves comfortable with the Mennonite tradition and finally found the South Seattle congregation.

"Do you have good relations with your parents?"

"Yes, but they think we're fanatics," said Barbara.

Ken Kraybill grew up in an independent church in Marietta, Pennsylvania. His grandparents had become unhappy and left the Mennonite Church, but Ken in turn reacted against the fundamentalism of the church in which he grew up. He came in contact with Mennonite Brethren at Fresno, California, then went to Goshen College where he

met and married Beth, a member of the Hively Avenue
Mennonite Church in Elkhart, Indiana. They came to Seattle for adventure and found "the first really close fellowship
we have been in. After six months I have grown very fond of
the people," said Ken, "the social conscience, the worship:
simple and contemplative."

Beth added that "we felt challenged by trying to fit faith
into city living. Last Sunday," she continued, "was
membership Sunday with people joining and various statements of faith. Though not yet ready to make that
'membership' move, I feel I have committed myself as much
to this church as to any."

Sylvia Mierau was back in Seattle for the second time. She
had grown up in a Methodist church in western Kansas, but
in college put the idea of church out of her mind. After
graduation from Wichita State, she got a job with the
United Way and met her first Mennonites. Indeed, she met
her future husband, Tim Mierau, who was a Mennonite, but
also not active in the church. They married and came to
Seattle for Voluntary Service, working for Seattle Mental
Health. "We were told that South Seattle congregation was
very open," she said, "and would accept people who did not
want to go to church."

"It was good to have the church for some marital stability
when working for the Mental Health Agency where marriage was not held in high regard. I was not worried much
about Mennonite identity, and when Tim wanted to go to
seminary at Elkhart, Indiana, I did not expect to be involved. But they really took me in. They got me involved
and I became part of a K-group (fellowship group). It was at
this time we became interested in the question, 'What does
it mean to be Christian in a violent world?' We got some
insights we wanted to hold to and were interested in coming

back to Seattle because of the church and because Seattle is a wonderful place to be."

I asked this group along with Lauren and Janet Friesen whether the South Seattle congregation is able to minister to the poor. The answers moved toward an appreciation for the Mennonite style of life and manner of service. As for the poor, Beth Kraybill said, "You don't just pick a group and say, 'I will relate to these.' You try to be authentic yourself."

More specifically Lauren told of congregational participation in an emergency feeding program. Each month they make up three or four food boxes which are used in a program for those in need. He also observed that "a number in the church have chosen lifestyle as an issue. Some have deliberately chosen lower paying types of jobs. Even some who have the better paying jobs live a simpler lifestyle than their peers."

He told also of Bruce Bowersox, a Quinalt Indian who heard of Mennonite work with children in the city of Seattle "and wondered if we had some Mennonite volunteers available. He saw us as trying to provide service with care and quality. That's what speaks loudly in a day when many groups are going for the 'sell.' "

The group consensus was that the Mennonite Church has found a way of responding to needs, an opportunity for involvement on a broad basis, not just a few specialists. "I think a lot of persons are concerned about hunger," said Sylvia. "I think my church was when I was growing up. But we didn't know how to carry it out. I think that Mennonites seem to have a better understanding of the problems of the deprived."

Barbara was pleased that among Mennonites if you don't have money you can still help. "Where I was raised, people are more well-to-do. My parents would give to the missionary fund, but you don't live a missionary lifestyle yourself. In contrast Mennonites make it possible for you to be involved. It has made a difference in our eating habits."

Ken recalled, "As I grew up I kept hearing the term 'full-time Christian work!' I have not heard this term among Mennonites. They seem to have been better able to integrate work and faith." Ken was employed in a mental health agency and felt that although he was not a pastor, he too was "in full-time Christian work."

Dave appreciated the attempts of Mennonites to dispel the American myth of consumerism, the belief that prosperity is the sign of the blessing of God.

Dave and Barbara were scheduled to go to Princeton, New Jersey, in the fall where Dave would be enrolled in Seminary. They wanted to visit Mennonites along the way and Mary and I felt it necessary to warn them that not all of us have reached the lofty ideals that they were appreciating.

Hisae Hatch actually did find South Seattle by invitation of one of the members, but she was prepared beforehand by reading. "I was raised in a Christian home in Japan, but when I came to America I went to many churches and was disappointed. Then while studying medieval history at the University of Washington I read about Anabaptists in *Mennonite Quarterly Review* and thought it would be nice to see a church like this. I did not know there was a Mennonite church in Seattle, but I met a Mennonite student and he invited us to his church. We started to come and they are very open. We like the caring part. Sometimes I feel Mennonites stress the denomination too much, but I think Mennonite teaching is close to the Bible."

Her husband, Wesley, added, "One of our earlier impressions was that this church did not have the obvious evidences of wealth."

Jim Mentzer, a propulsion technician for the Boeing Company decided one day that he had been in Detroit long enough and moved to Seattle. A friend gave him Lauren Friesen's name. "It was a very off-the-wall situation that brought me to Lauren, but the first thing that happened with the church was that Lauren took me to camp. I immediately felt at home and this has kept me here 3½ years. Another thing that impresses me is that they take a stand on important issues and try to carry out some of them. The future will be very interesting as I am planning to get married and my fiancée is not Mennonite. Church will be negotiable. We will probably experiment. If she feels uncomfortable here, we will find one where she is comfortable."

Would no one say anything critical of South Seattle congregation? Miriam Leatherman of the positive word had one qualification. "If I were to voice any dissatisfaction, I think we should have attracted to the congregation some non-professionals in a city where there are so many." She did note several members who work with their hands. Though educated Tim Mierau, however, works as a carpenter and Darrell Graber is an auto mechanic. "But we have nobody who is just a high school graduate."

South Seattle sponsors two Voluntary Service units in Seattle in cooperation with Mennonite Voluntary Service at Newton, Kansas. VS is a feeder for the congregation. It was suggested that at least a dozen of the members were formerly in VS. One of these is Randy Elston, the first to serve in Voluntary Service in Seattle, in 1971. He and his wife, Mona, had recently returned to Seattle to reside there more permanently.

VS persons in Seattle normally work in social service jobs, and are paid at the level of United States VISTA volunteers. As Lauren put it, their availability "permits an agency to get

Ann Marchand, ministerial intern at South Seattle. She finds Mennonite worship too unstructured, but enjoys the close community.

more or better staff than they could otherwise."

Only two of the current group were Mennonites, although those we met seemed dedicated persons. Among them was Ann Marchand who had recently become a seminary student intern under Lauren's supervision with a view to attending Mennonite Biblical Seminary in Elkhart in the fall. An article about Ann by Peggy Kilborn Newcomer appeared in *The Mennonite* on February 5, 1980. As a devout Catholic, Ann found much at South Seattle to cherish, but not all. "Once or twice a week Ann ends daytime activities with 5:30 p.m. mass at St. Joseph's Catholic Church. 'This is important to me,' she explains. 'Mennonite worship is so unstructured. I miss ritual and liturgy. I think also that Catholics put more emphasis on meditation and prayer, and I need this reinforcement. But,' she continues, 'there's no sense of community at that worship. For that I go to the Mennonites.' "

As much as any congregation we visited, South Seattle has attempted to be all things to all people. "We have a variety of backgrounds," said Lauren. "Catholic, Episcopal, Greek Orthodox, Assemblies of God. We don't press them to reject their background, but wait for them to make a choice."

Yet anyone from those traditions who attended the meeting the Sunday we were there could not fail to recognize that it was a Mennonite service and not the one they came from. Seats in the old supper club were arranged in a U-shape. There was singing, Scripture reading, a story for the children, a Scripture meditation, prayer requests, and informal sharing. Rod Schmidt, a medical student, gave a report of research on which kinds of canned tuna contained more and less lead. There was plenty of coffee and tea for all.

It was a church, but also a family. Which was it more than the other? Who could tell?

14
A New Opportunity

"I observe that in most of our churches we have four strong emphases. These emphases give us identity as a people. They are study, fellowship, service, and worship. They cause us to be a people of the Word, a people of community, and a people of mission, and a people of peace.

"Evangelism is doing for others what we have done for ourselves.... The saddest conclusion I have reached in recent years is that the world is far more eager to hear the Word of God than the church is to proclaim it."

The speaker was Palmer Becker, recently resigned as Secretary of the Commission on Home Missions at Newton, Kansas. The audience was the Conference of Mennonites in Canada gathered in annual session. Among the people were members of a committee seeking a pastor for a new congregation forming in Richmond, British Columbia. The vision of the speaker was impressive.

Gerd Bartel remembers the situation. "The next day my dad said, 'Have you asked Palmer to be your minister?'

" 'Oh,' I said, 'don't be ridiculous.'

" 'Why not,' he said, 'you can't lose.' "

Palmer Becker, pastor of Peace Mennonite Church. "Evangelism is doing for others what we have done for ourselves."

So although he was not a member of the committee, Gerd spoke to one of them and the eventual result was that Palmer Becker became the pastor of a church not yet formed with a building only on the drawing boards.

But the story is really not that simple. What was to be named Peace Mennonite Church in March 1980 was to grow out of the intentions and traditions of two, no three, Mennonite congregations in greater Vancouver. Thirty percent of the 4,300 members of the Conference of Mennonites in British Columbia live in this area. Except for the Chinese Mennonite Church in Chinatown, Vancouver, a large majority of the members have come through migrations in the nineteen twenties and after World War II.

In *Churches in Profile*, a publication of the British Columbia Mennonite Conference, the membership of the Sherbrooke Mennonite Church in Vancouver is described as follows: "30% were born in Russia, 23% in Paraguay, 18% in Canada (12% in British Columbia), 11% in Germany, 4% in Brazil, and 5% in other countries. The diversity in background and experiences has enriched the fellowship."

Sherbrooke is helping to sponsor the Peace congregation in the mother-daughter fashion. It is supplying cash toward the cost of the new building and providing members on a self-selected basis to help comprise a congregational core. The result is to take pressure off the Sherbrooke facilities and also spread the witness. One criterion of selection, no doubt, is geographical. A number of Sherbrooke families live in Richmond, the site of the new church. A Vancouver suburb, Richmond has a population of 100,000, twice what it was 10 years ago.

A second sponsor is Prince of Peace Mennonite Church, a small congregation formerly located in Richmond which found its members dwindling and so threw itself and its resources into the new effort. Gerd and Regina Bartel were members at Prince of Peace and represent the more recent migration. Gerd was born in East Prussia where his father was a prosperous farmer before World War II. Regina was born in Munich of parents who were refugees from Russia.

Gerd told of how it was to come to Canada after World War II. "We lived in an area that was nonchurched and non-Mennonite. I was the only Christian kid in my high school graduating class." It was not the most auspicious time for German Mennonites to seek to enter a British-oriented culture. "It wasn't pleasant being the only one in school wearing leather shorts," Gerd said.

But Canadian antagonism did not keep the German Mennonites from working and prospering. Gerd's grandfather had earlier helped a man emigrate to Canada and when the Bartel family came this man helped them get farms. The Mennonite refugees arrived in a country of rich resources in the process of rapid development.

"As a group Mennonite refugees have been 'way too successful,' " said Gerd, a high school mathematics teacher. "I have relatives who 15 years ago were laborers and today they are independent millionaires. They got into building and farming at a crucial time. Farmers in the chicken business have become millionaires in 10 years."

Though it is indeed significant that Mennonite refugees have become prosperous, they are part of an area that appears generally well to do. One reason Richmond and other outlying areas of greater Vancouver are developing so fast is the pressure for cheaper housing by an expanding population. By "cheaper" housing, according to Gerd, is meant $30,000 for a 33-foot lot and $100,000 for a modest-sized house. Wages, of course, are commensurate. Two wage statistics quoted to me were $12.00 an hour for a starting carpenter and $29.00 an hour for automobile service.

The result of this population pressure is to urbanize the country. The land in Richmond never should have been built on, said Palmer Becker. "It's garden land, some of the best land in North America." Yet the lots were being filled up rapidly. The Beckers lived in a new house on a spot sold them by a family who moved their house to the side of their lot so they could turn part of their high priced land into liquid assets.

The Sherbrooke congregation owned a church-sized lot in Richmond and made it available as a site for the new meetinghouse which would seat 350 and was projected to cost $700,000. This price was well beyond my concept of what a local church would be expected to spend on its building, but as mentioned above, Vancouver is a high cost area. And they pointed across several blocks to a Mennonite Brethren plant which they said had cost $2 million.

One hundred and forty thousand dollars was going into an auditorium/gymnasium attached to the church. The idea of a church with a gym was also new to me, and I discussed it with Ken Kehler, secretary of the steering committee which was responsible for organizing the new congregation.

Ken replied that the original vision for the auditorium/ gym had come from Erwin Cornelson, former pastor of the Sherbrooke congregation. One concern was to have a place large enough for wedding receptions which evidently are quite large among the Mennonites of Vancouver. Ken told of his own wedding where 600 were served at a sit-down meal and it required three "settings." So the pressure is on to rent a school or another hall and "the temptation is to have other non-appropriate activities enter in. Already before the building is finished," Ken said, "families are asking to schedule it for weddings.

"The initial vision is to have this facility available for celebrations. The word 'gym' crept in because some saw athletics as an outreach." He noted that "there has been difficulty in getting a time slot for boys' and girls' clubs in the

Gerd Bartel (left), from the former Prince of Peace congregation: "I hope we can have at least some of the same sense of community we had at Prince of Peace." Ken Kehler (right): "The Peace Church will provide an opportunity for us to serve in outreach, but I know this is where we will be weakest."

regular church facilities and this will be a place for these."
He hoped too that "the auditorium will be a place to invite
people for films and musical programs." He said also that
the "only way for people to know about a larger church
family is to do things jointly" and observed that "we can
entertain the British Columbia Conference, the Canadian
Conference, Mennonite Central Committee, the General
Conference.

"One issue that is still on the surface is, How many dollars
should we spend? I can justify it, but does it please God? It
won't please all our members, for there are some bitter notes
coming through."

The gym, it was pointed out, is a shared project and will
be owned jointly by Peace and Sherbrooke. Other Mennonite congregations in the city will be welcome to use the
facilities and to become partners also if they wish.

I noted that in what seemed on the outside an enormous
building, the worship center was limited to about 350
people. Why this limitation in size? Ken indicated that it was
a major decision of the steering committee to keep the
membership size down. Presumably when the worship
facility filled up it would be time to form another congregation as Sherbrooke had grown out of First United Mennonite in 1968, and Peace was coming from Sherbrooke in
1980. Indeed Palmer Becker reported that Peace has in mind
to start a daughter congregation in five to eight years.

One of the issues that comes up, however, in this sort of
congregational self-selected swarming is what kinds of
persons leave and what kinds stay. The tendency seems to
be for younger leaders to leave. Thus First United Mennonite of Vancouver which has given birth to three different
congregations, now has 60 percent of its 600 members over
the age of 60.

In March 1980 some had declared themselves as members at Peace and others had not yet decided. But already some of the ambivalent feelings were there. When I mentioned the option to Jake Braun, choir director at Sherbrooke, he said of Peace, "They are too strong already."

Some older people were going to Peace. I spoke to Eugenie Dyck, a widow who felt limited in her use of English and agreed to be interviewed only when I promised to ask no complex questions. I wondered why she would be transferring to the Peace congregation. "My children go there and also I am old and live close to the church. I was brought up in German, but I think I'll feel at home because my children are there." I was told also of Gerhard and Elisabeth Klassen who were joining Peace. Elisabeth was taking English classes in order to understand better.

For Peace would be going a step beyond Sherbrooke— there would be no German language worship service at Peace. When one ponders the makeup of the Sherbrooke congregation described above, one can see why the German language would not be dropped without careful thought. Indeed, Gerd and Regina Bartel reported that they spoke both German and English to their preschool daughter in order that she might grow up as bilingual.

Ken Kehler and his family were transferring to Peace from First United Mennonite where he had been ordained as a lay minister in 1976. He felt some sense of being a deserter, but he told how he got involved with Peace. He had been designated to serve as a substitute for Pastor David Nickel when the meetings which led to the organizing of Peace first began. One thing led to another and soon he was a member of the steering committee. He found it fulfilling some personal yearnings.

"I began to realize I was a part of something new. It was

not long before I saw this would meet some of my own needs. The language was one thing. As our children were growing up, we saw that we were not fostering the German language. Another was my wanting to experience a small group. (I've always been a part of a large church.) Also, it is an opportunity to reevaluate the role of the church in the community. At First United Mennonite the church, because of its size and the language barrier, was basically serving itself.

"I long for an opportunity to become involved with people and yet it frightens me. The Peace church will provide an opportunity for us to serve in outreach, but I know this is where we will be weakest. I chose to serve in the area of outreach because though I have fear, I feel this is where I want to work."

I asked Gerd and Regina Bartel about their expectations for the new congregation. Since they had come from the small Prince of Peace Church, they hoped to be able to preserve some of the values of a small, innovative congregation. "I hope we can have at least some of the same sense of community we had at Prince of Peace," said Gerd. "This is the only church experience we have had in our 13-year marriage and we were both totally involved. It was more than a congregation; it was a family, and we hope this may continue."

Regina hoped that "people will be open to novelty and not say right away, 'We never did it this way before.' I want the worship service to have a certain amount of reverence. Good quality music and a concern about the words as well. As for children, I'd like them in the service."

Gerd remembered too that Prince of Peace had had a team ministry with four preachers who took turns. He was one of the four. "Here I learned to speak. A lot of us feel we would like to have lay people involved, but others want a pastor to preach. I would say let's not have people speak who have nothing to say."

They recognized that it would be necessary to allow for a wide representation of viewpoints. "Some of us who are keener on these kinds of activities will need to hold back. For example, some of us thought we should form the church first rather than erect the building. But others thought it better to erect the building first and assume that the church will come. We from Prince of Peace have sold our building and spent a year and a half as transients!"

Palmer Becker also has an interest in the church functioning as a caring community. His solution is to organize the local congregation on several levels. "Something happens in groups of 12 or less," he said. "If the church is to be a place where people care about one another and discern gifts, this happens best in groups of 12 or less."

"It seems to me another thing happens in groups of 40 to 60. This is about the size of group you can learn to know well, for example, in a retreat.

"Again something happens in groups of two hundred plus. One pastor can 'shepherd' this many people if he's got good deacons. When you get beyond this, you've got a conference.

"What I think we need to do is to develop leadership for all of these levels. I'm no longer scared of 1,000 members if you've got leadership to look out for the groups of 12 and the groups of 50."

He showed me a sketch of the organizational pattern for the new congregation. As planned, the church council would include the congregational chairperson, pastor, and secretary, plus nine elders, each of whom would be responsible for one area of congregational activity, or as the planning

document put it "who will give direction to major areas of
ministry. At its beginning these shall be worship, study,
fellowship, finance, property, and probably deacons." This
seems to care for the organizational life of the congregation
though it may be a little top-heavy for a congregation expected to begin with about 100 members. But what of the
smaller units mentioned above? The units of 12 are covered
by the following statement: "To develop a warm, spiritual
dynamic in the church, each elder shall lead (or be in training toward leading) a small group of not more than twelve
persons where there is sharing and prayer together with
some elements of study and mission."

It appears that the persons in the small group would not
necessarily be those for whose work the elder is administra-
tively responsible. Thus as envisioned, each elder has both
an administrative and a pastoral responsibility.

For the groups of 50, Palmer said there had been talk of
having a deacon lead a group comprised of three small
groups plus additional persons, and have each of these units
meet once a quarter. It seems a carefully thought through
organizational structure and one wishes them well as they
explore it.

I asked Palmer what surprised him upon taking the
assignment as pastor of the group which later chose the
name Peace Mennonite Church. His first response was "I
was surprised to see tradesmen at work; their efficiency and
vigor. After 20 years of experience they can work really well.
It was a jolting and helpful experience to compare this with
how I function in the ministry." He also mentioned being
"surprised at the apathy of the neighbors, good people who
feel they don't need the church."

From a church planting standpoint, Richmond is an area
of need. Palmer estimated that the church buildings in Rich-

mond would provide seating for 15 to 17 percent of the
population. There is negativism about Christianity as his
daughter Jo found in a high school class. The teacher
asserted that both science and Christianity have failed and
we must now turn to humanistic philosophy. The whole
class seemed to cheer and Jo felt really alone. But then she
spoke to the teacher and he agreed not to ridicule her in
public. She also later found one other Christian student in
the class.

So the Peace people appear to have a wide open opportunity. This is what attracted Palmer to the assignment as
pastor of the congregation. "I really wanted a church where
there was an opportunity to win some people for Christ," he
said. "It seemed to me this provided the best opportunity of
the places we explored."

I asked him how the congregation expected to appeal to
Richmond with the gospel. He responded in line with his remarks quoted at the beginning of the chapter: "Doing for
others what we have done for ourselves, in Bible study,
recreation, and service. The first concern will be for
unchurched relatives. Almost every family has them."

The people of the Peace congregation, as described by
Palmer, have "a strong concern for evangelism and service.
They want to be known as honest and hard working and in
business, if they say they will do something, they will."

In a very short time these traits have made them accepted
and prosperous members of the Vancouver business community. Will the people of Richmond be willing to join with
them also in the worship of God and the search for the
meaning of their congregational name? No doubt the
members at Peace are aware that this is a much more difficult and delicate assignment than even coming to terms
with the economic rules in an alien culture.

15
The Family as Church

"There are three major families in our church," said Joe Kauffman. "Kauffmans, Birkys, and Lapps. Almost everyone is intermarried." In addition, the 95-member Mountain View Mennonite Church with its meetinghouse in an open field of the Flathead Valley near Kalispell, Montana, was the most rural congregation we had yet visited on our tour of North American Mennonite congregations. After a long list of cities and suburbs, we were pleased to find a country church that had not yet been discovered and swallowed by a city.

And it did seem to be a family type church. Though I did not have time to verify Joe's comment, I perceived a complex of relationships: brothers, sisters, aunts, uncles, cousins, and grandparents. On Easter Sunday morning as I viewed the congregation, I saw a representation of the various age-groups, though perhaps not as many older people as one would expect.

"The reason in part," said Pastor Glenn Roth when I raised the question with him, "is that a lot who would now be older people disassociated themselves from the Men-

nonite Church at an earlier time." He spoke of a period
when church standards and discipline were such that some
persons simply left. In the Flathead Valley there was no
other Mennonite Church for them to transfer to as they
might have done in a more populous Mennonite area.

Isolation from other Mennonites is a problem Mountain
View has lived with from its beginning in 1913, 10 years
after the first Amish Mennonites moved into this fertile
valley in northwest Montana, just beyond the Rocky Mountains. There were 20 charter members when the new building was dedicated on September 20, 1913. The new congregation was named the Mountain View Amish Mennonite
congregation.

These facts are taken from a book by S. G. Shetler entitled
*Church History of the Pacific Coast Mennonite Conference
District,* published by Mennonite Publishing House. As
described by Shetler, one of the congregation's early problems was affiliation: where could it find a Mennonite district
conference close enough to make association reasonable?
"The congregation was organized under the Western Amish
Mennonite Conference," writes Shetler "and in 1915 asked
to be released from this conference in order to unite with a
conference geographically nearer."

Mountain View was released from the Western
Conference in an action taken at a session in Missouri, more
than 1,500 miles away. It then joined the Pacific Coast
Conference, of which the nearest congregation was at
Nampa, Idaho, more than 400 miles away. Finally, in 1923
Mountain View was released from the Pacific Coast
Conference and joined the Alberta-Saskatchewan
Conference, somewhat closer geographically and with a
yearly farming cycle more nearly like that of the Flathead
Valley. Today it remains a member of this conference, now

Clifford Brenneman, church council chairman at Mountain View Mennonite church and one of two full-time farmers remaining in this congregation with a meetinghouse out in the fields.

called "Northwest." It takes its turn hosting the annual conference assembly and members participate in conference activity. The week of our visit Church Council Chairman Clifford Brenneman had traveled to Calgary, Alberta, for a meeting of the Commission on Missions and Service, of which he is a member. He reported that the commission was hoping to establish a mission church in Great Falls, Montana's second largest city.

The farming cycle is less an issue now than formerly. Though the meetinghouse is out in the fields, less than a majority of Mountain View families is engaged in farming. In a meeting of 15 or 20 people, I asked how many had grown up on farms. Two thirds or more indicated they had grown up on the farm, but they said only two in the church are now full-time farmers, although additional persons live on the land or gain a part of their income from farming. When I asked why the change, Paul Kauffman mentioned that the high price of land had eliminated some from farming. Instead, members work in logging, sales, and the professions. Some are laborers and Duane Clemmer, who had been trained as a computer programmer, worked in a fast-food restaurant because he had not been able to find work to utilize his computer background.

The loggers were out of work because of spring breakup, and they weren't sure how soon the activity would begin again. The lumber industry was hurting because high interest rates had slowed house building and thus softened the market for lumber. "The lumber market is terrible now," said Ezra Birky.

Regardless of how they felt about employment in the area, the Mountain View members were unanimous in their praise of their geography and climate. It helps to keep them there and bring them back when they go away. "I was in

Eastern Colorado in 1953," said Joe Kauffman, "and they had practically a dust bowl. It didn't take long for me to get enough of that. My wife is from Iowa and they have nastier weather than we." He added that outsiders also are being attracted to northwest Montana. "We're getting an influx of people from Colorado and California because they like our beautiful country."

It does seem beautiful country. The mountains are in almost perpetual view not only from the meetinghouse, but from all over the valley. In April there was snow on the mountains. I asked Clifford Brenneman when the snow melts and he thought in early June. Duane Clemmer, who married a girl from Kalispell and moved from eastern Pennsylvania, said, "The only thing I miss here is the leaves changing color." (Most trees in the nearby mountains are evergreen. However, there are aspens and cottonwoods, but their leaves turn only pale yellow in the fall.)

Northwest Montana is not only beautiful, it is large. Indeed, Clifford Brenneman expressed the conviction that Flathead County is as large as the whole state of New Jersey. However, it can't compete with New Jersey for population. Its total is about 40,000, of whom more than 25 percent live in Kalispell. At 11,000 it is the seventh largest city in Montana. But even here there is population pressure. Jeff Buller reported that "people are building houses so far up the mountain they complained to the forest ranger that the bears were bothering them. He replied that in reality they were bothering the bears."

To be rural is not, however, to be delivered from life's seamier experiences. At the time of our visit an area resident was on trial for the murder of his wife. Such news was less than reassuring to Mary Brenneman, widow of former minister Daniel Brenneman, who lives alone in the country.

So she appreciated having Neil and Dorothy Yoder living in a mobile home on her farm. Neil and Dorothy moved to the area from North Dakota. They had considered moving on to Oregon but "the Lord hasn't led us to Oregon yet. So we will stay here for now." Mountain View folks are concerned to function under divine commission.

One feature of their congregation they reported with satisfaction was the number of persons who have served in an alternative to military service or in church-sponsored Voluntary Service. It goes back at least to Civilian Public Service in World War II. No precise statistics were cited to me, but Marjorie Birky asserted, "We have one of the highest records of I-W and VS. Ever so many of the kids have served."

One who served was Allen Stutzman, a Paxman for two years in Zambia who then came back to Kalispell. "It was a real shock to return," he said, "but here it was home. At one time I was disenchanted with the church, but I got married here and that settles you down. There are problems in the church, but it is very alive. The basics of what ought to be there are there. I see a lot of things I think are good."

Mountain View seeks to relate helpfully to its geographical area. One way is to support the local volunteer fire company. Daniel Brenneman and his son Clifford were charter members. One feature they helped to initiate is an annual sale as a means of fund raising. We were present at the time of the sale, and it was reported that the women's auxiliary had netted $9,000 from their activities. The proceeds from the farm machinery and household goods which were sold at auction, mainly on consignment, were not yet available. Four men from the church were currently members of the company. Allen, one of the four, sees it as a "good opportunity for Christian witness."

Other service activities mentioned to me were Paul Birky's work with prisoners (I wanted to interview him, but failed to make contact), and sewing by the Womens Missionary and Service Auxiliary, ("If somebody 'burns out,' we give them a comfort," said Mary Brenneman), and the Browning project. This has been an ongoing program of relationships with Indians across the Rockies at Browning on the Blackfoot Reservation. It has been done since the early seventies in cooperation with the Voluntary Service division of Mennonite Board of Missions. Mountain View has an elected committee which serves the VS group with supporting counsel. The congregation takes one offering a month for the Browning unit.

The committee and the VS group had breakfast together on Easter morning and discussed developments in the program. I talked with the director Steve Amstutz about the work. He described the situation in Browning and the unit's attempt to be helpful. "There are incredible amounts of money and programs available to these Indians, so much so that some young people don't bother to work. There are four or five churches in town, all white led and the businesses have mainly white proprietors." The function of the VS unit is to try to help put some meaning in life. High in the emphases are boy's and girl's clubs and a recreational center. Once a month the unit shows films, alternating between those that might appeal to children and films for adults. Attendance suggests that these are appreciated.

An earlier project recalled by Ruth Stutzman was a yearly applesauce canning activity. Women from Mountain View traveled to Browning to help Indian women can applesauce. "Ray Horst said this was one project we shouldn't drop. But we did."

One might imagine that in a congregation so filled with

family members, those who have no relatives would feel left
out. There was some evidence for this. Elma Mast, for
example, mentioned that she and Mary Brenneman used to
"chum together" after Mary's husband died because neither
one of them has sisters in the congregation.

But I met a number of persons who had not grown up in
Kalispell and who yet seemed to feel quite at home. Some, it
is true, had married persons from Mountain View. Marjorie
Birky came from Hubbard, Oregon, and when her husband
brought her to Mountain View, she found some congregational emphases very different. "But I put my letter in right
away and was used." The Birkys pioneered by adopting
interracial children and "there were some problems in the
congregation. But it's getting better. It wasn't until Joe
Kauffmans got their little Indian boy that things opened
up." (Joes reportedly had taken their 16th foster child.)

Duane Clemmer from the Line Lexington congregation
in eastern Pennsylvania met his wife in Voluntary Service in
Columbus, Ohio. Since she was from Mountain View, they
moved there after service. I asked him to compare the two
congregations. "This is a smaller congregation and so there
are no direct comparisons. There is a lot of potential for
growth here. I think there are people who are working for
growth, not necessarily in numbers, but in spiritual growth.
The congregation here is like a family—everyone knows
what is going on everywhere else. It's a different experience
because my wife knows everyone and I don't, but I'm getting acquainted."

So far as I could tell, neither Menno Troyer nor his wife
have relatives at Mountain View. They moved to the area
from Hartville, Ohio, so Menno could work for the forest
service. Menno was from the Hartville Mennonite Church, a
large congregation, and he found the tempo at Mountain

View quite different. But he was grateful to the congregation. "They took me in."

Another who found a home in this small church is Ray Bush. After the Sunday morning meeting at Mountain View, Mary went out to take pictures. I finished my contacts and was ready to leave, but she continued talking with someone in an auto poised to go. It was Ray Bush and he was telling her about how he grew up at Johnstown, Pennsylvania, and performed alternate service in Ravenna, Ohio.

Here he learned to know Mary's father, Eugene Yoder, and when he decided to move West, Eugene gave him a *Mennonite Yearbook* in order that he could locate Mennonite churches in the areas where he went. He used it to find a Mennonite minister in Denver, Colorado, and later to locate the Mountain View Church in Montana. Pastor Glenn Roth recommended him for the job he now holds, and Ray is a member at Mountain View. "A lot of the people came to help us move into our house," he reported.

Mountain View people took satisfaction in telling how their present frame building was not only built with largely volunteer labor, but a good bit of the lumber was furnished by the Birky sawmill. Also as reported by Ezra Birky, "We have never had a janitor, families take turns." Sometimes it is almost more than one family can handle. His wife, Marjorie, remembered "cleaning until we felt goofy. Once we worked 22 hours to get the building in shape."

Pastoral service also is basically free, though the congregation provides support toward Mennonite Mutual Aid Retirement for Glenn Roth and pays his way to leadership retreats. He supports himself by a combination of a small farm and carpenter work.

Traditionally Mountain View had a plural ministry. A recent leader in the congregation was Daniel Brenneman

who was commissioned for Mountain View by the district
conference in 1943 and served there until his death in 1975.
Ministering with him until 1966 was John Hochstetler who
moved away that year. In 1969 two younger men were ordained: Duane Oesch and Glenn Roth, but in 1971 Duane
was called to Minot, North Dakota. Thus since 1975, there
has been only one minister. But there is now a church
council of six men and according to Pastor Roth "it works
better." This representative group helps to share responsibility for decision making.

The discernment process at Mountain View has been affected by the changing experience of the members. Now
that they pursue diverse occupations, as Wayne Lapp put it,
"there is less of a set rule about what you should or should
not be involved in."

Also, according to Joe Kauffman, "VS has done a lot for
the congregation in broadening perspectives."

But as there is change, there is tension. Some have left,
Paul Kauffman reported, because "they said we are drifting.
I guess we are." Marjorie Birky was concerned that the congregation remain Mennonite. "Some have said we ought to
have a community church. I say if we have a denominational church it ought to be Mennonite."

Yet in addition to these statements of concern, there were
various appreciative comments about what the congregation
has done for or meant to the members. Anna Birky reported
that her husband, Elmer, "had surgery in Seattle and we
were gone a month. We had mail every day."

Wayne Lapp said, "One thing I appreciate is I am part of
a membership that cares and allows me to care."

On Easter morning the Sunday school gave a program
which included a skit by one of the children's classes,
assisted by a grandmother. In the play the class visited the

grandmother to invite her to attend their Easter program. The grandmother demurred because of previous bad experience with the church and utilized some of the usual clichés against Christians. The teacher responded as follows: "That's true to a point and I wish I could tell you that our church is perfect, but it isn't. Christians aren't perfect, just forgiven." The grandmother reluctantly agreed to attend the program.

This opening scene was followed by Scriptures, songs, and readings. Then the class and the grandmother met again and the grandmother was converted. She said, "I really enjoyed your program and especially the children and the expression on their faces. I never realized before that so much depends on us. I'm so glad the children invited me." A little simplistic perhaps, especially since we had met the grandmother the evening before and it seemed clear that she already loved the Lord. But it signaled a Mountain View intention.

I saw what appeared to be a significant number of young adults and young married persons at Mountain View. In light of the dropout stories we have heard in other congregations, I wondered about their presence and asked a young couple, Ken and Frieda Kauffman, for their perception of Mountain View.

"The church is starting to move," said Ken. "There's a bright future here. Some of the little 'picky' things will change. It used to be that when problems developed people would move away. Now they stay and face them. We tried to move three times, but were stopped each time."

Frieda added, "The last time we got the message, 'Go home and tell what good things the Lord has done for you.' We have had the baptism of the Holy Spirit."

I asked Glenn Roth to tell his vision for the future for

Mountain View. "To touch this community and have people become a part of the church. I feel it is going to happen because members are showing concern for each other. Persons from without are coming to our meetings. Others are asking if they could come. We have a very needy area. Ministers in the Kalispell Evangelical Ministerial Association agree that there is no conflict between churches. There is work for all."

On August 30, 1964, Mountain View met to dedicate the meetinghouse where they now worship. The litany of dedication is printed in a program which was given to me. It reads in conclusion:

> *Pastor:* For a testimony in this community of the saving and transforming powers of Jesus Christ, for a bulwark in the nation, to be a defense of righteousness, and to give a Scripture witness against all types of evil.
>
> *Congregation:* We now dedicate this house to the Lord our God. We the Bishop, Deacon, Pastor, and people of this church, do here and now dedicate ourselves anew to the worship and service of our God.

Who of us is sufficient for such a great dedication? Yet every church should have a vision greater than itself. At Mountain View they are recognizing that it is not enough to be a family church with brothers and sisters, aunts and uncles and cousins. If they are to be a family of God in the New Testament sense, they need also those who belong simply on the basis of faith in Christ and intention to follow Him.

16
A Church on a Hill

The Bridgeway Community Church sits on the brow of a hill in Swift Current, Saskatchewan, where it can be seen from all directions. When you get closer, there is its name on the front and underneath it the mysterious letters "M.B." Insiders know the letters stand for Mennonite Brethren. People new to the church scarcely notice them.

The name of the church "is our attempt to deal with the ethnicity problem," said pastor Peter Nikkel. "When people hear the word 'Mennonite' they think of bonnets or long black clothes. In our church we want to break free. We are not trying to reach just our own people. We want to go back to the Anabaptist spirit—they were evangelists—but still maintaining separation from the world."

The Bridgeway name was chosen in 1977 at the time the congregation moved to its new meetinghouse. Before this the congregation was simply the Swift Current Mennonite Brethren Church. John Penner, chairman of the building committee, came to Swift Current in 1956. He recalled that at that time the congregation had a small building that seated 80 to 100 people. In 1959 they built a church that

The Bridgeway Community Church building in Swift Current, Saskatchewan, can seat 600 and includes a gymnasium/banquet hall.

would accommodate 250 people. The new building can seat up to 600. John thought the congregation had grown as much as 40 percent in the three years since the move, "especially if we count the 29 new members to be received on May 4, 1980.

"I think we have been able to penetrate into the not traditionally Mennonite community," he said. "I think one thing that contributed is our high visibility. We took advantage of every opportunity for publicity." Indeed for a time Bridgeway had the largest meetinghouse in town. It cost $600,000 even with many hours of volunteer labor. The plant includes a gymnasium/banquet hall which is used for congregationally sponsored club and athletic activities. Extensive catering is also done by volunteer groups in the congregation. It is the only church in Swift Current with such large facilities for serving meals and there are regular calls for its catering services.

"We are getting a lot of people and they are quite comfortable here," said John. "As soon as we get new people coming, the pastors conduct a 'Christian basics' class during the Sunday school hour. The class runs almost continuously. Once people have accepted Christ and talk about joining the church, we explain Mennonite doctrine."

Not all the new people have come to the church since the new building. Jill Cavanaugh accepted Christ in 1975. Jill had grown up in another denomination, but evidently faith was not a serious matter for her. Peter Nikkel's little boy came to her kindergarten class. She was sufficiently informed to know that Mennonite meant "religious" and she had the opportunity to discuss with Peter the difference between her religion and his. Peter replied that (1) he was a pacifist and (2) for him being a Christian was not only a Sunday thing. He told her how to make a Christian commitment and assured her that she would be welcome at his church at any time.

Eventually the time came when she made a commitment and determined that she would go to church the next day. "I wasn't sure what the Mennonite religion was like, and I didn't know about adults attending Sunday school. When I got there at 11:00, the lot was full of cars and I thought I was late. I sat in my car and wondered whether Mennonites wear hats in church.

"The Lord must have been pulling because I went alone. I thought I was late and I wasn't sure what to expect. When I got inside, a lady came and introduced herself and asked if I wanted to sit with her." For Jill this was the best kind of welcome she could have received.

Jill's involvement with the church put some strain on her marriage. "For the first year my husband accused me of going to church because I got so much attention. Yet at crucial times he has been very encouraging. When I was to be baptized he said, 'Don't be afraid.' He supported me when I spoke at a Christian Business Women's meeting. He has been encouraging when the pressure is on though he doesn't like it when I get involved with the church. I like to share my testimony and tell stories about exciting things that happened to me. This is easier than to be patient with my husband."

It was three years before Jill was baptized and her spiritual development continued after this. "It was just recently that I quit smoking," she told me, "and only recently that drinking is not important to me. For a time I did not go out with my husband because I couldn't say no. But now I can do it, although I don't really enjoy going to parties. They seem a waste of time." In return for Jill's going to parties with him, her husband began attending Bible study, but he confessed that he couldn't take it.

An open, frank person, Jill is surprised when others are less free. "I've been told that my approach to Christianity is open and honest. This puzzles me—I wonder how you can be otherwise. As part of my testimony in church I said that I had tried to quit smoking and failed. I know that others in the congregation have this problem, and I don't understand why more of them don't share it. For me this was helpful. The thought of dear old Mrs. Martens praying for me helped to get me stopped. I couldn't let her down."

Jill summarized her experience with these words: "My strongest statement for accepting Christ is that my life now has discipline which it did not before. I am really enjoying discipline."

Not only does Bridgeway reach out to people of Swift Current. Its arms are open to Mennonite Brethren from other areas as the Cliff Jantzens found when they moved from Lanagan, Saskatchewan, for Cliff to accept a position in the regional department of education. "When the assignment opened we thought it important to see what the church was like. So we visited Bridgeway Community Church and were welcomed there. It helped to influence our decision to come to Swift Current.

"We found in the church a number of intermarried family groups and we wondered if we could break in, but our initial impression was confirmed. We have never had so many invitations to dinner."

The congregation also found in Cliff a person who was willing to be involved and within two years he had been elected chairman of the elders and congregational moderator. From this position he reflected on some of the issues before the church. "There is a danger," he observed, "that in our church professional, intellectual, or occupational abilities may be the criteria for influence rather than the guidance of the Spirit." He hoped "that everyone in the church will be recognized for the contribution they can make. Otherwise we are building on a shaky foundation."

A second concern was similar. "That we do not rely too much on the pastors to do the work for us." He had full respect for Peter Nikkel and the associate, Neil Block, who had come only the year before. "But it concerns me that he is doing tasks formerly done by people in the congregation." He noted also that "until now most of the follow-up contacts with people having spiritual needs have been Peter's work. Lay people have not been sufficiently involved in this front end of evangelism. Until we are, we will not reach our potential."

Neil Block is Bridgeway's first associate pastor and it is his first pastoral assignment. He indicated that the job description had been purposely kept fairly loose. "We agreed to let the job develop, and it has. I am quite free to move from emphasis to emphasis," though one special emphasis was to be evangelism.

"But I had a little frustration. When they called I was told they were looking for someone to work in evangelism, but when I came I found the pastor was already an evangelist. So I find that I am trying to assist him by becoming personally involved with people."

Two tasks that Neil assumed which others had done before were leading the choir and leading the young people. But he indicated that the latter was one of the temporary assignments. "There seemed to be no one available as youth sponsors, so it was agreed that my wife and I would serve as sponsors for 18 months to train some others. But I was glad for the opportunity to work for a time with the young people."

As he came to know Bridgeway Community Church, Neil was particularly interested in two groups: (1) the older people and (2) the young adults.

"The senior people are very supportive of what has been happening in the evangelistic emphasis. I am amazed at how gracious they are." As for the young adults, "they were coming along with the church, playing a strong role in reaching out to people their own age—people who were hurting."

We found the opportunity to meet representatives of both of these groups. (John Penner and Cliff Jantzen, of course, represented the group in between.) Ed Loewen was cleaning the church the Saturday we were there. A retired farmer, he and his wife moved to Swift Current in 1974.

"My wife and I thought we would retire from church activity and take it easy, but it didn't happen." In 1975 they became janitors of the former building. Ed was elected as chairman of the board of deacons and served until he said there should be a younger man. In the new building there is more custodial work and the deacon work was curtailed by the custodial work, so there is a second couple. "But at the end of the year we are going to throw in the white towel."

He invited us to lunch in their apartment across the lot from the church. "My wife and I have always been busy hosting people." When Mary protested that an hour was too short notice for his wife to prepare, he said, "Oh, it's no problem. We have leftovers from last evening." Leftovers or not, it was a more tasty meal than some we had eaten in restaurants.

I asked about the deacon organization and their work. He indicated that deacons look after the communion service, visit members in their homes, and provide spiritual counseling. "We have four deacon couples and one sister. We have been asking for at least six couples. I asked the pastor, 'What is it that frightens young couples away from being deacons?' I realize they are busy with their jobs and families. But maybe they see it as too exalted a task. I read Timothy before I consented and asked my wife whether we could do it. She said, 'We can't, but the Lord will help us.'"

He described the visitation system as follows. "All families in the congregation are divided into groups and each couple is responsible for a group. My wife and I try to see our people two or three times a year, but there is one couple I see once a week." The groups are newly formed each year.

Another older person was Helen Thiessen, a widow and the "sister" Ed Loewen had mentioned. She referred to herself as a deaconess. She and her husband had retired in Swift Current in 1973 and he died within the first year. He had been a Mennonite Brethren pastor, although blind, and Helen had provided support as a pastor's wife. When he died, she had to reassess her life, and Bridgeway served as the context for this. "I have been happy at Bridgeway," she said. "Peter is tops. He's sensitive and God-fearing and dedicated, interested in souls. Did he tell you we are having a baptism again, 18 people? A lot of it is Peter's work. Perfect strangers come to his office."

As a deaconess, Helen is a pioneer. "I think this is the first time one of our southern Saskatchewan churches had had a deaconess. When I was asked I said, 'If I am required just to visit the widows, I won't do it.'" But she was assured that instead she should continue to do the kind of work she had been doing before. Only now it would be formally recognized by the church.

The idea of a woman in a prominent position of leadership is new for Bridgeway and occasional questions arise. "Two years ago the Christian Endeavor decided to

have the women bring the program on Father's Day and I
gave the message. Peter is very conservative about this, but
he went along with it. The program was on Sunday evening.
I don't know how it would have gone on a Sunday morning."

Ron Kuehl, thirtyish, represented the younger group. He
had moved in from Ontario just as the church came into its
new building. He and his wife had no relatives in Swift Current, so they became the "adopted couple."

"It was a good six months before we had some time to
ourselves because we were invited out for so many meals."
Ron observed what several others had mentioned, that moving into a new building did not immediately change the congregation's mind-set. They were living in a large church
with a small church mentality. "We've got the facilities.
What do we do about them?"

He said the "breakout began with some non-Mennonite
people coming to the church, professing faith, and getting
involved. This helped people to see that we really are a community church. Further, a group of 9 or 10 persons our age
got together and organized a young adult fellowship. This
has grown to about 60 with one couple serving as overseer of
the group. There are Bible studies once a month, sometimes
twice, and fellowship at least once a month. The fellowship
nights provide a place to bring people who are on the
fringes. Say a wife has made a commitment and her husband has not. He can come to this without pressure."

Ron reported also that the concern of the group goes beyond talk and good fellowship. "Someone can be in difficulty and a call goes out for help. One fellow's union was on
strike and he was falling behind in his mortgage payments.
The word went out and his payments were caught up
without his knowing it."

Ron Kuehl: "When you place yourself in a demanding sport, your witness is on the line."

Another activity Ron mentioned very positively was the church hockey team which included not only persons from within the congregation, but also "some sports-minded fellows who have not made a commitment. We have gotten together 40 times with these fellows over the winter. When you place yourself in a demanding sport, your witness is on the line. You're not the pastor or a deacon, you're a hockey player. I know of two on the team who have found the Lord."

What is expected of people who come to Bridgeway? The qualifications for church membership stated in the constitution include confession of personal faith in Christ Jesus and evidence of new life, baptism by immersion, "a teachable spirit in matters of faith and Bible interpretation," willingness "to conform to the lifestyle described in the Mennonite Brethren ethical guide, and . . . to accept the standards as established by the church." I did not see the Mennonite Brethren ethical guide, but a congregational confession of faith distributed at the time of the dedication of the new building included the following: "We believe that Christians should not be conformed to the world, but should follow Christ in every area of life. They should refrain from force and violence in human relations and show Christian love to all men."

As may be expected, the emphasis on love in place of violence can be an issue for some. But according to Ron Kuehl, "Mennonite beliefs like nonresistance are no big thing. Some of us have said that in no way will we defend the country. Others said, 'If you have a yellow streak like that, okay.' "

It was reported that Bridgeway is a well-to-do congregation, but generous in giving. "There was a time when I dreamed that I could sometime touch a millionaire," said

John Penner. "Today I come to church and rub shoulders with millionaires every week, farmers tilling from four to six sections of land. If they own even a portion of that they'll be worth a million." He acknowledged, however, that inflation has destroyed the meaning of millionaire, for a farmer might have $500,000 invested in equipment to do his field work. But as one involved with the building project, he was grateful for the support. "God's been good to our people in financial ways and I think they have responded in return. When we started this project, we had some qualms, but we never missed a payment."

Ron Kuehl characterized Bridgeway as a friendly church. "If you walked into church on a Sunday morning, you would feel at home because they welcomed you." And so they did. A man we had not seen before appeared from somewhere and invited us to a Sunday school class. During the worship service which followed, Peter Nikkel introduced us to the congregation. Others spoke to us later.

By earlier appointment I had a quick interview with Richard Weetman and Glen Gutwin, leaders of the Boys Brigade, a church-sponsored activity program with games, projects, and Bible study. We had seen the boys on Saturday collecting soda pop bottles in the area around the church. They informed us that they had collected $400 worth of bottles and that the proceeds would be used to send boys to summer camp.

The brigade is organized in two tiers—one group age 8-11, and the other 12 and up. They were pleased to report that seven of their boys were scheduled for baptism in a few weeks. "We think we have something to do with it, though they have a very dedicated Sunday school teacher."

Our final contact at Swift Current was with Larry Schwiethale, manager of a local restaurant. Larry told us a personal story amazing in its complexity. He had moved to Canada from the United States with his second wife to get away from support of a first wife, from whom he was divorced, and their children. For seven years the first wife kept pursuing him for support, so he put all his assets in the new wife's name.

"We became very successful, she in her business and I in mine. We had over $90,000 in automobiles alone and a very large bank account. Then my business declined and I needed more capital. My wife wouldn't turn over any to me and on September 1, 1979, she informed me that she was leaving. The bank said I must put in more capital and the word came that my father in the United States was ill with cancer.

"I was crushed and contacted the mental health clinic, but they would not see me without an appointment. So I went to Bridgeway Community Church where we had attended occasionally. Neil Block did not pressure me, but gave me some literature. That night I accepted Christ and the miracles began."

Among the "miracles" Larry mentioned was an advance of capital by a Christian man from whom Larry had once stolen. "I called him and told him what I had done. He and another Christian advanced me some capital with no guarantee except that I was a new creature. I dedicated my business to the Lord and returns have increased 48 percent over this time last year."

He went to the United States and discovered that his former wife, his daughter, and his former mother-in-law had become Christians. He met his former wife at his daughter's home and "we spent four or five hours confessing things to one another. During the course of this, we prayed for my present estranged wife." Larry showed us a letter he received later from his mother-in-law "who had never before accepted me." She wrote "everything you are going through now is helping to prepare you for a glorious future. Keep your eyes on Jesus. With every temptation, he will make a way of escape."

A divorce from his second wife was pending, but a disagreement postponed the settlement until the end of the summer. "At this moment my covenant with God is that my present wife and I stay together. The Lord has something planned for the next five months. I have found complete peace with myself and it is directly the Lord's doing."

"Evangelism is a high priority," said Peter Nikkel. "We want to be a mission church."

Larry Schwiethale would say that he is glad. "The biggest thing that brought me to this church was the openness and friendliness, their concern."

17
A Church Without a Church

On the morning we were to visit the Fort Garry Mennonite Fellowship, I overheard students at Canadian Mennonite Bible College talking about the fellowship. A snatch of conversation went something like this.

"They're radical . . . and rich."

"No. Charleswood is the rich one. If they were rich, they'd have their own building."

As much as anything, the lack of its own facility sets Fort Garry apart from the other 26 Mennonite congregations in the Greater Winnipeg area of Manitoba. Since early January of 1967, the fellowship has met for worship in a double classroom of the Canadian Nazarene College. Henry Goertzen found it. "We decided to try to find a place," he recalled. "I think it was God's leading. I went over to the Nazarene College and said, 'Maybe this is going to sound silly, but could we work together? You use it during the week and we on Sunday.'

"He said, 'It's not silly at all. I have been following your movements, and will be glad to work with you.' "

By the spring of 1980, the lack of a building had become

an issue. Not a crisis issue necessarily, but one on which people expressed divergent opinions when interviewed separately. And in the mind of Delores Lohrenz, it had blunted the willingness of some to speak freely in fellowship meetings. As Delores described the background, a church building was available at a good price and a majority wanted to buy it. But others asked for time to explore other alternatives and the moment for purchase passed. "Some became very unhappy and some of the openness left. Not much was said but at the next few council meetings people did not speak as freely, though nobody left the fellowship because of it."

Henry Loewen explained his reservation about the church that was for sale. "I guess a number really wanted it; they thought the shape didn't matter. But there are pews in that building!"

His wife, Cora, added, "If the pulpit is at one end of the building, that's where it's going to stay."

Henry indicated that some attention has been given to a design for a new building which would be in line with their own convictions. "In the design worked on we tried to avoid creating a focal point other than the center of the congregation."

A case for a building was made by Henry Goertzen. "Our children come into a classroom and seldom enter a church. I don't think they get the reverence."

Abe and Verna Hiebert also hoped for a building. "I have hoped for at least ten years," said Verna. "Whatever we put on the wall for Sunday school, we have to take off. There is no room to put anything away. Even the social committee has to drag home the mugs and tumblers."

Henry and Grace Rempel conceded that there probably would be a church building in the near future. "I think there is a feeling that something has to be done, regardless of what it is. I think we will be building a church," said Henry.

He observed that there seem to be three groups in the congregation. One would like a more traditional church program with a building. A second group likes the status quo; or at least does not see a church building as important. A third would like more radical church settings—house churches or intentional communities. "I predict that we will get a new church building, then draw in more people. We will then move to a part-time professional pastor, then a full-time. Then house fellowships will be facilitated within the church."

Another possible development he envisioned was the forming of a separate Fort Garry type of fellowship out of the larger congregation once it was "on its own. But you can't talk about it publicly."

As implied by Henry's remark, the lack of a professional paid pastor is another mark of Fort Garry's distinctiveness. It seems they did not set out to seek the pattern of leadership they now have. Anne Goertzen recalled that "we had really intended to have Larry Klippenstein as pastor, but he got a scholarship and moved away."

"Then Henry Epp came in," her husband, Henry, said, "and he was much for the shared ministry."

The concept of leadership developed at Fort Garry over a period of some years is called "multiple team ministry." It is described in the congregation's covenant booklet in terms of a covenant "that we will build the local congregation by assigning tasks to each other. This will be known as the team ministry. We will all need to assist each other and study how to work together." Three teams are specified in the covenant: a planning committee, a worship committee, and a Christian education committee.

No one is ordained to serve in the Fort Garry Fellowship. Instead all are called and those who accept specific assignments are commissioned. One result of this approach is to press all into service, regardless of age or sex. Fort Garry has about 75 members, so all are needed to perform the ministries for the congregation. As Anna Ens put it, "It is hard to get lost in our church."

The teams include women. "I think our congregation is very good to women," said Delores Lohrenz. "I don't realize it until I talk to women in other congregations. The nominating committee called and asked me to let my name stand for congregational chairman. I was astounded and at first I said 'no.' Then I told my family and I found that my children said 'yes!' I think you would not find another church in all of Manitoba where you could do this."

At some point in Fort Garry's development it was agreed that their three committees did not provide for all the functions needed in the fellowship. So was evolved the office of "lay minister." In the bylaws the statement on lay minister notes that "our belief in the priesthood of all believers places all members under a commitment to serve each other. Nonetheless, there are several functions that we recognize as performed better within the context of ordination. In particular, lay ministers are to be available to perform baptism, marriages, and funerals within the Fellowship." It is expected that there will normally be two lay ministers. They are elected for three-year terms and may succeed themselves once.

In spite of the term "ordination" quoted above, the lay ministers are not necessarily ordained in the formal ecclesiastical sense, but rather commissioned for the duration of their terms. The official head of the congregation is the chairman of the planning committee who also serves as moderator of the whole.

Henry Loewen, a school administrator, was nearing the end of his second three-year term as a lay minister. He displayed a mild ambivalence about the responsibility implied in the term "lay minister." But he found comfort in the models of leadership he had observed in the past. "I always had very good experiences with the church leaders. They came into our home and I knew them other than when they were thundering in the pulpit."

For him it was at first a novel experience to serve communion as an ordinary member of the congregation. "That was a big thing. I came from a tradition where the bishop did it. The first time I was asked there was a question whether it would be meaningful to me or for others. But our practice has been that anyone may serve communion."

A recent discussion brought about a broadening of the lay minister's responsibilities. As reported by Bernie Wiebe, one of the two, "Now the congregation is asking us to step out more in the prophetic leadership role. I have probably been one of the pushers for this, not because I wanted to do it, but because I thought we have not challenged one another enough." As examples of the new role, he said, "Once a year there is to be a time of goal setting led by the lay ministers. Also they are now automatically named as members of the planning committee."

Even with this broadened responsibility for lay ministers, there is still a kind of loose endedness in the fellowship's organization and functioning. Anneli Braul, who grew up at Fort Garry, prefers this to the problems of the alternative.

"I like what the church is trying to do. It is not always successful, but I have seen quite a few problems with the professional minister. He has to do everything for everyone. He has to compromise his convictions because it is one man against the council. Also, it gives more incentive since each person is needed. I would choose the loose ends because you can always work at that."

Is the Fort Garry plan a model for others to follow? According to Henry Rempel, only if their situation matches Fort Garry's. The key is the availability of gifts and a willingness to be used. The question, he says, is "Are there within the members sufficient resources in preaching and teaching to do the job?" He also thinks it is a model especially for "couples of a certain age. All of us are of a fairly similar age. There are a few old couples and some younger ones," but he implied, not as high a proportion as the middle-aged.

I had talked with Henry and Anne Goertzen, somewhat older, and discovered their needs as different from the Rempels. I spoke also with several younger, unmarried persons. Gayle Wiebe, a first-year university student, said, "I like it a lot—the way I got involved right away. Now I'm Sunday school teacher, church pianist, children's choir director, and on the music committee. I am welcome at all the meetings. I went thinking I would be out of place, but found I was accepted." Now that she teaches Sunday school, she can see the point of a new building for the Sunday school and the youth group. "But I wouldn't vote for a pastor. I like the present system."

Gayle told of comparing notes with a friend who attends First Mennonite Church in Winnipeg. "She likes her church and I like mine. She says she likes going to church and seeing all those people. I like going to church where I know everybody."

Allen Harder, veteran of Mennonite Central Committee service in Zaire and Uganda, was more tempered in his praise. "I had very high expectations and the experiences were not always positive. But I still think I would rather stick with this congregation. I think the church does try to integrate the unmarried more by intention than action. In this church things are not overt; they just tend to happen."

He recognized, as did some others, that different groups have conflicting priorities. "Quite a few people need to have a structured program and others want the priesthood of all. An additional group has a third need. Some of us are talking more in terms of intentional community."

Economies on building and local program enable Fort Garry to give more generously to outside causes. They take satisfaction from their ability to maintain a 60/40 balance: 60 percent of their money for outside and 40 percent local. Of the local 40 percent half is used for operating expenses and the rest goes into a building fund and reserve. They are pleased with their ability to meet their conference and mission commitments. "Some congregations in Winnipeg have never met their conference obligations," reported John Friesen. "We have never missed ours."

Fort Garry treats the giving of money along with the giving of time in the stewardship section of its covenant: "The temptation to live for self and luxury is so great that we will encourage each other to give at least the minimum biblical tithe (10%) as an expression of devotion." The 1980 budget called for $32,000. For 75 members this is an average of more than $400 per member. According to *Yearbook of American and Canadian Churches* it puts them well above the average of the conference of Mennonites in Canada at $332.89, but well below the Seventh-Day Adventists at $756.67.

Their money is raised without great fanfare. An offering is taken only once a month. But Abe Peters said, "My preference is to do it once a year. Then when a special appeal comes along, I can give some extra."

And what of Fort Garry as a place for children? "It's the

only church they've ever known," said congregational chairman Willie Falk concerning his own family.

Bernie Wiebe observed that after his family had been away from the area for five years, there was no such thing as considering another congregation. "I think a part of it is the strong family intimacy. We work hard at a solid Christian education program and family activities. We also try not to schedule things that tear the family apart."

Henry Rempel philosophized on the experience of younger persons at Fort Garry. "What does it mean for them to be a Mennonite? In larger churches it is to join a choir. This does not happen in our small church. For ours it becomes attending a Mennonite school, summer camp, a bicycle tour, conference activities."

I sensed that an important document for the Fort Garry Mennonites is their covenant. It was referred to at various times as a source of guidance for congregational life. Delores Lohrenz told of how it was developed "through intense, lengthy discussion. Each part was decided in open meetings."

Her husband, John, spoke of the benefits of the covenant: (1) giving direction to new members; (2) guidelines for decision making; (3) used in the instruction of the young.

Sometimes I have heard that the process of developing a statement is as important as the statement itself. What now takes the place of the process? They responded that the process is ongoing. The discussion on baptism took two years. Other subjects requiring extensive time were lay ministry and nonresistance. The section on house churches was not yet complete. "We thought we would say our covenant is never finished," said Delores.

And what about local outreach, ministry to and bringing in people from beyond their immediate families? The lack of

Fort Garry Mennonite Fellowship on an evening out. From left: Dorothy Adrian, Bernie Wiebe, Delores Lohrenz.

our own building is a limitation, said Willie Falk. "We have not been part of the community. There is a visible evidence."

However, "most households have outreach," according to Abe Peters. "Quite a few people get involved through school and community committees, as coaches in soccer and baseball, as school program volunteers. On our street there has been a Bible study group across denominational lines. My wife has been involved for many years. In an urban setting, outreach takes many forms."

Willie added, "The problem is to put it all together so that we can support each other."

One specific outreach activity of the fellowship has been to sponsor a Vietnamese family. "They are formally members of the congregation," said John Friesen, "but are also associate members of the Mennonite Chinese Church in Winnipeg. They feel closely related to us because we have sponsored them, but they receive their spiritual nurture more from the Mennonite Chinese Church. They attend our meeting in the morning, and the other in the afternoon."

He acknowledged, however, that "we really have not drawn in non-Mennonites. It may be partly due to the fact that we don't have our own building. But we have a number of Mennonite churches in Winnipeg who are very evangelistic and they haven't won anybody either. Every ethnic group in the city has its own church. Of course, there are also many nonchurched people, but we have not been able to persuade them."

Abe Hiebert seemed to speak for the fellowship on this issue when he said, "Directly our church membership doesn't show much influence in our area. But I think that indirectly we have a lot of influence."

Like a number of other congregations we had visited, the

Fort Garry Fellowship seemed poised on the edge of a new era. As John Friesen summarized it, "There is a growing feeling on the part of some that we should move to a professional pastor and among others that we should have a facility. Some see these as problems to be overcome; others view our present situation as theologically a good approach."

It was reported that an architect had been engaged to draw some building plans. There was also conversation about inviting some persons from the Bethel Mennonite Church in Winnipeg (which was feeling pressure on its facilities) to join with Fort Garry in order to relieve pressure at Bethel and provide a wider base of financial support for a new facility. But this prospect raised uncomfortable questions. "Maybe we've solidified our positions and would be threatened by 20 families moving in and saying, 'Why do you do it this way?' " remarked Willie Falk. "Could we handle that?"

At the time of our visit, plans were being made to organize the fellowship for the new church year. Marge Wiebe reported for the nominating committee. "I made a lot of phone calls. Some of the people are really struggling about whether they should let their names stand or not. It was interesting how many yeses came very, very quickly. And some people who said 'no' had legitimate reasons."

It sounded like a typical report from a nominating committee, though perhaps a little more positive than one would expect. But then this is the congregation which believes in the opportunity and responsibility of all to serve all. Even such dedicated people must occasionally feel a little weary. As Anne Peters remarked, "It might be nice not to be on a committee for a year."

18
The Little Church
That Grew

Steinbach, Manitoba, is a town of 6,000 people with 16 churches. Ten of these are Mennonite. It is only fair that Mennonites should predominate in Steinbach. The town was founded in 1874 by 18 families of a Russian Mennonite group known as the Kleine Gemeinde. Today this church is called the Evangelical Mennonite Conference and has its headquarters there.

During the week the United States failed in the attempt to rescue its hostages in Iran, we went to Steinbach to get better acquainted with the Evangelical Mennonite Conference and especially its Steinbach congregation. Our hosts were Dave Schellenberg, editor of the EMC publication, *The Messenger,* and his wife, Helen.

As I learned from Dave, and from sources provided me, the EMC began as a renewal movement among Mennonites of Russia following Napoleon's invasion in 1812. According to Sue Barkman in *Ever-Widening Circles,* a history of EMC missions, the Mennonites of Russia felt so good about their 40 years of privilege in that country that some of them wanted to contribute to the Russian war expenses. But

"Klaas Reimer, a layman, vigorously objected to this new interpretation of nonresistance as well as the lax leadership and nondiscipline in the church."

A few people followed him and his little group was dubbed "kleine gemeinde" or "little church." It was hard going for the little group. Opposition from without and dissension within kept their numbers down. By the time of the mass Mennonite emigrations from Russia in 1874, there were two groups of Kleine Gemeinde. One came to Nebraska, and the other to Manitoba.

John Holdeman, who had led a renewal group of his own in the United States, visited the Manitoba Kleine Gemeinde, and perhaps a third of them joined his Church of God in Christ Mennonite Church. For 50 years those remaining ran a holding operation, but in 1924 youth meetings began and in 1925 Sunday school. In the thirties and forties the Kleine Gemeinde began looking outward. In 1953 five congregations in the area around Steinbach made up the conference, and they organized the Board of Missions.

This was a year after a name change: from Kleine Gemeinde to Evangelical Mennonite Church. (In 1960 the name was modified slightly to Evangelical Mennonite Conference of Canada.) In October 1979, Dave Schellenberg could write in the *EMC Yearbook* that "EMC membership has increased in Canada about 50% from the early 1960s. Present membership is around 4,800 in 46 churches." He noted their distribution from east to west: "Ontario—2, Manitoba—29; Saskatchewan—9; Alberta—3; British Columbia—3."

In the same *Yearbook*, Board of Missions Executive Secretary Henry Klassen could report 130 career missionaries, and 38 short-term workers. Of these about half were serving with mission boards other than the EMC. These persons were considered associates, and were given some support by the EMC board even though they did not serve in the board's program. The EMC-sponsored mission activity is found in Canada, Germany, Mexico, Paraguay, and Nicaragua.

I asked associate mission secretary Milton Fast about his vision for the future of their program. "We are aware of the need to build a stronger support base in Canada to support the foreign work." (One can understand this. Henry Dyck, pastor of the Steinbach EMC, reported this congregation's quota for missions at more than $200 per member per year.)

Milton also expressed concern about the need to break out of the Mennonite family ghetto. "We have for quite a while been asking why we don't have other than 'Mennonite' names in our churches. But this is beginning to change. In northern Manitoba and Winnipeg you see people of other nationalities coming in. I'm thinking we are beginning to break that barrier."

I obtained a list of the family units related to the Steinbach EMC and noted a sprinkling of names that did not appear traditionally Mennonite. I showed these to Dave Schellenberg and he indicated they were the results of inter-marriage. At any rate the Evangelical Mennonite Churches in the Steinbach area have been growing. I made brief contacts at three others in addition to Steinbach and all four have had to consider how to respond to pressure on their facilities.

Steinbach had formed a second congregation, Kleefeld was erecting a new building, Blumenort had just decided to put up a larger auditorium, and Prairie Rose was considering whether to remodel, build new, or hold two services.

"Our membership is almost totally natural," said Pastor Edwin Plett of Prairie Rose congregation. "There are strong family ties. The parents have been strong with the church, and the young follow them." Having good employment opportunities helps. "Geographically we are not too far from the city of Winnipeg and from Steinbach (in both of which jobs are quite readily available). They don't want to live in the city, so they stay here." But keeping them active in the church is not done without some effort. He told of leading a study group with three couples: two of them Mennonite men with Catholic wives and the third a Mennonite man engaged to marry a Catholic.

With memberships of more than 500, Blumenort and Steinbach were some of the largest congregations I had contacted on the tour. How would such large congregations function? Not, according to Pastor Henry Dyck of Steinbach, by having the pastor visit every family every year. "I have been trying to educate the church to understand that the minister can't do justice to preaching, teaching, and counseling if he tries to visit everybody once a year." He considers this concept a romanticized view of the pastor's work. Instead, he "would rather see people minister to one another."

As an alternative, the members have been divided into seven groups with an "associate minister and a deacon responsible for visitation and ministry." This program was somewhat new and evidently not yet functioning smoothly. But "one group had a potluck and did brainstorming as to how they could minister to one another."

In place of the Wednesday night prayer meeting which was a dying "sacred cow" when Henry became pastor, they now have Bible study groups which "involve more than half of our people." But scheduling is a problem. "My main dilemma is getting together with people in such a complex society where moms and dads and teenagers work. How do you visit when you have to do it all in the evening? A Bible study group I lead meets at 9:00 p.m. I have to do a lot of late contacts like this."

To the visitor, Steinbach seems a friendly, unhurried place. But according to Henry Dyck, "Unrighteous mammon is really throwing a lot of weight around. My concern is for my people to be biblically oriented, so I preach less topical sermons, and more Bible outline types—such as going through the Book of Romans to familiarize them with it. I want the Bible to come alive for them."

Steinbach EMC also has a full-time youth director, Jim Harms. A former truck driver, with a handshake like a vice grip, he and his wife, Angela, were both comfortable, but unsatisfied. Instead they were called to Steinbach to put some stability into the youth program. His responsibility as he sees it is "to try and work the youth of our church so the young person can see 'I am important and the church needs me.' " He refuses to serve as a liaison between parents and youth. "When young people come with a family problem, I send them back to their parents. If they still can't agree, I will get involved."

What kinds of problems do they bring? "Parents treating them unfairly. They can't understand the standards. Fourteen-year-olds think they are old enough to set their own standards."

His emphasis, in working with youth, "is to meet them where they are and establish common ground. I have felt very comfortable with their feelings toward me and the church. There are a few petty negative feelings, but nothing strong." In fact, he was concerned that for some of them the socialization process could be too easy. "Our youth seemed to feel that growing up in a Christian home and going to church automatically made them Christian. But they are beginning to recognize that one is not a Christian just because his parents were."

A dream of his is "that we may be able to hold our young people and challenge them to keep involved in a fellowship of Christians and see their responsibility to the community, to their families, and to the nation as Christians. Another dream is to have the entire youth population of the church involved in the youth program."

Lest we think that all is at rest in Steinbach, I should report that I also attended a Bible study/prayer meeting of adults from Steinbach, and some requested prayer for their "unsaved children." The path of family life has never been completely uncluttered.

I spoke with several laypersons in the Steinbach congregation beginning with C. P. Loewen, president of Loewen Millwork, reported to be the largest employer in Steinbach. He was also chairman of the board at the church. "I feel I have tremendous support in the church," he said. "In the past a conservative element in our congregation was not overly happy about business people, but I have not felt this for years. The duties of a person in business apply in all of our lives."

What kind of sermon helps you most?

"I like any sermon that is Bible centered and I like to have an application made to today's living. I also like to think I am most helped by a worshipful sermon. We sometimes forget the great God we have."

Ellis Penner is a turkey raiser. Three years earlier he had left a position in a real estate office to raise turkeys—four flocks of 9,000 each from March to November. "I had a good job with a pension plan, but my boy wanted to be a farmer. Deep down I did also. That's how I started looking around, first for a hobby farm. Then I ended up with this. I enjoy it very much, though I'm not saying I wouldn't go back to real estate."

I learned that his family was transferring to the Blumenort congregation which is closer to the farm and where the children can have the same companions at school and at church. What do you expect from the congregation? "I told my family, 'Let's not expect. Let's give.' There is a tendency for us to take churches for granted. I think the best is the opportunity to serve. The new congregation is in the same conference, but it is different. Yet we find it a friendly church."

Coincidentally Art and Mary Reimer had sold their farm to Ellis Penner and were now operating a mama and papa grocery store. "Sometimes we feel really blessed in sharing Christ with people who have serious needs," said Mary. On the other hand, "Some customers aggravate me and I have to go out back and pray for patience. I think the Lord is teaching us a good lesson."

I asked them about changes observed in the church in their time. Art replied, "Changes are quite plentiful, particularly in the line of 'missions.' It is completely different from 30 years ago when mission work was almost frowned upon. A few had to break the ground. They were considered rebels and some never did see results, but we reap the advantages."

Mary added, "Some of our people thought the less we know, the less responsible we are. Ben Reimer [an older member of the Steinbach congregation] said he was told not to go to Bible school lest he learn too much."

What are the issues today?

"I'm almost afraid we have reached a pinnacle and are self-satisfied," Art replied. "Then in our society we have so much money. That's hard on our young people."

Ellis Penner describes the finer points of turkey raising to Dan Hertzler and Dave Schellenberg.

The problem of affluence. How many leaders in the area had mentioned it?

Dave Schellenberg: "We are generally quite concerned about materialism, affluence."

Henry Dyck: "Unrighteous mammon is really throwing its weight around."

Ed Plett: "One of my goals is that as a church we may be able to keep priorities straight with regard to materialism—to react to it in a Christian way and adopt a lifestyle that reflects our values, ministering within the community and beyond to the deprived."

John Loewen, pastor at Blumenort: "There is always a tendency in a time of affluence to become materialistic and complacent, and lose the meaning of life, to build a little nest for ourselves."

The area seemed like a good place to "build a little nest." Blumenort, according to John Loewen, "is a growing community. Industry brings people in. Others are retiring and coming back to the old community." The towns of the area are tidy, the countryside well manicured. Dairy farming is common and the profile of the A O Smith Harvestore silo is seen throughout the land. At one farm Dave Schellenberg and I noticed five of these big blue structures. We asked how many cows there were on this farm: one hundred fifty? Three hundred, our source replied.

What other problems would there be in such a pleasant place? "Becoming acculturated," said Ed Plett. "Social drinking is being accepted too well. Also I have some difficulty with the openness to movies. I believe they have an influence. Another issue is marriage and divorce. Three couples of the Prairie Rose church have been separated and the wife in a couple interested in joining the congregation was formerly married and divorced. I think also the whole emphasis on sports is divisive at times."

But Ed was not giving up. The issues would be faced as far as he was concerned. "One of the things I am hoping is that we can reach out and draw into our community of faith people moving into our area. We may need to let some cultural practices go. Not Anabaptist theology, but some of our favorite foods."

Several of the congregations have sponsored Vietnamese families and at Blumenort there is a Vietnamese program once a month with a Chinese pastor who comes from Winnipeg. Also there is a ministry to the deaf, spearheaded by Jake Driedger, who has three deaf children. There is "signing" for the deaf at morning and evening services and once a month a program for the deaf from other areas.

What about the ministry of women in the Evangelical Mennonite Conference? I asked Dave Schellenberg. "It is not really an issue," he said. "There are no women on conference committees or congregational councils. However, there is now a woman on the congregational mission board at Steinbach." (The responsibility of this board is to process candidates from the congregation interested in serving with the conference mission organization.)

There is also an active program among the women in support of Mennonite Central Committee. They were preparing used clothing for shipment to Akron, Pennsylvania. Though supportive of Mennonite Central Committee, the Evangelical Mennonite Conference considers itself more "fundamentalist" than certain other Mennonite groups, especially the General Conference. (No doubt also there are still memories of the Great Church which persecuted the Little Church in Russia.) But in the General Conference, as Henry Dyck observed, "there were some 'liberal tendencies' from which we shied away. We don't want to tell the state what to do." But he pointed out that for themselves, they spell fundamentalist with a small "f."

That the EMC and the Steinbach congregation are serious about the church is revealed by the size of the budget. The 1980 congregational budget was $344,000, or about $625 per member. That seems on the upper edge for Mennonite giving.

Our last contact in Steinbach was a visit to the Mennonite Village Museum, a major tourist attraction. It was not yet opened for the season, but we got special permission to go through under the guidance of 80-year-old John C. Reimer, one of the leaders in its development.

What should be included when you set out to memorialize the past? Generally museums emphasize geography, housing, transportation, clothing, culture, and the tools of industry. At Steinbach it is much the same. There are, for example, three houses from the past: a sod house, a log house, and a Russian Mennonite house-barn. One end of the building was for the people and the other end for animals. Between the two were double doors in order to minimize the passage of odors from one to the other.

There is also a church building. Much of the interior of the building seems quaint by today's standards: gray painted open-backed benches, with one side of the room for men and the other for women. (You can tell which side was for men by the hat pegs above.) There is a wide platform in front. One side of it was for the song leaders, and the other for the ministers. Mr. Reimer wasn't able to say why the song leader's side was fronted by open spindles, and the other had a solid front. Nor could he account for the fact that in a church which emphasized brotherhood, the pulpit should be the most elaborate feature in the room.

But on one matter he was clear. The joists for the low ceiling were as heavy as barn timbers. Why such heavy construction in a church ceiling? For the storage of grain. And why store grain in a church? As a reserve for those who might be in need during the winter.

So there it was again: the caring community. If there was to be one theme which surfaced repeatedly during this tour it was that Mennonites are people who care. No longer will the sign of caring be barn timbers in a church building. Indeed, it may be that Steinbach needs to work harder at defining for this time what shape the caring should take. But in the Mennonite collective memory is the experience of concern for one another. It is a memory to cherish.

(**In Conclusion**)

What More Shall I Say?

The writer to the Hebrews had to stop his account of heroes in chapter 11 because, he said, the time ran out for the telling. Indeed, time is often too short for the things we would like to do. One of the frustrations of this project was the need to pass by more congregations than were visited because of the shortage of time. Indeed, this is the reason for some lack of consistency in the reports. Certain chapters cover a number of congregations lightly instead of one in more depth because in setting up the study I could never quite decide between breadth and depth.

Now that these stories have been presented, is there need to say any more? Certainly not very much lest the quick witted should read the conclusion first and then skip the whole book. But I have gathered that some feel such an experience should have taught me some things definitive about the Mennonite Church. As early as the halfway point on the trip, requests began to come for a report of my observations.

What I have learned has been presented in the chapters of this book, so only a few more things will be added, some general observations that came to me as I reflected on the project as a whole.

I was impressed by the variety of cultures represented in these Mennonite congregations. I was impressed, but not exactly surprised, for I had met black and Latin Mennonites before. The route followed was chosen in part to expose us to a variety of groups. Having made the trip I am reassured, for I believe the church must be able to transcend cultural and tribal barriers. "Once you were no people," Peter wrote to those whose only claim was faith in Christ, "but now you are God's people." It is the faith that counts, more than the background.

I was interested, furthermore, in the varieties of practice found among these congregations. In some the ministry of women was accepted and encouraged—in any role. In others, women served only in certain types of assignments. Some of the younger congregations have written covenants which members who wish to remain in good standing are asked to sign every year. In another congregation, there is no signed membership list. Whoever attends and participates is considered a member. Yet both appear to be serious about their faith.

On the other hand, there are some things these churches appear to have in common. A noticeable common experience is urbanization. I think that more than 85 percent of these church buildings were in towns or cities. And in the country churches, farmers were in the minority. This means a wide variety of occupations.

As I recall the experience, the two most common problems mentioned were instability in marriages and the problem of money. Both make leaders uncomfortable, for they no doubt recall Jesus' stout words on both subjects. But in an open, affluent, hedonistic society, faithfulness in marriage and voluntary poverty are not popular doctrines. Given the trends of our culture, we may be grateful for the relative stability and faithfulness among us.

Indeed, what about the historic Mennonite doctrine of peace? Is this still believed in churches which are urbanized and have brought in people to whom this teaching is new? In various places I was encouraged. I was pleased by Jon Mumma in Chesapeake, Virginia, to whom peace was a new idea, but who was learning to accept it and was impressed by the worldwide network of Mennonites, even in Russia. I was interested when Eugene Arsineau in Des Allemands, Louisiana, encouraged me to publish more articles in the *Gospel Herald* on Mennonite history and doctrine and more teaching on conscientious objection to war. I was impressed too when Kevin Jordan of Inglewood, California, commented that people have been attracted to the Calvary Mennonite Church by its integrity and unique Mennonite doctrines such as nonresistance, sharing of resources, and covenant.

On the other hand, I had the uneasy feeling that not all members of these congregations would choose peace instead of war. Like marital faithfulness and the stewardship of resources, peace is a hard saying and not all are prepared to accept it.

I was encouraged to hear people say they had come into Mennonite churches because of the care and the sense of community they found. I am sure that not all of our churches have been successful in caring. I hear about this lack from time to time. But I found it reinforcing to be told again and again that a congregation had cared enough for people that they wanted to be part of it.

I met a number of younger married persons who at one time had been church dropouts, but had found their way back through the efforts of an enterprising pastor or an open congregation. These were among the more encouraging experiences of the trip. On the other hand I talked with concerned parents who had seen their children leave the Mennonite Church. How to interpret the faith and have it accepted by the next generation is one of those mysteries which the believers' church has never been able to fully comprehend. My observation suggests that congregations far from the young persons' homes should be alert to the opportunities to invite them to become active in faith.

Mary and I returned more encouraged about the Mennonite Church than discouraged. We know, of course, that the people we met were the convinced rather than the doubters. But even a critic such as Joe Wannemacher at Albany, Oregon, acknowledged that there was something good about the church. "I like the church," said Joe. "I'm stuck with it." And so are we.

Mennonite Congregations Visited[1]

Ch.	Congregation[2]	Begun	Group[3]	Members
1	Germantown 6026 Germantown Ave. Philadelphia, PA 19144	1690	GC, MC	29
2	Diamond Street 1814 West Diamond St. Philadelphia, PA 19121	1935	MC	49
3	Mt. Pleasant 2314 Mt. Pleasant Rd. Chesapeake, VA 23322	1905	MC	204
4	North Tampa 206 W. 131st Ave. Tampa, FL 33612	1927	MC	63
5	Des Allemands R. 1, Box 37-D Des Allemands, LA 70030	1937	MC	95
6	Houston 1231 Wirt Rd. Houston, TX 77055	1967	GC, MC	58

Ch.	Congregation[2]	Begun	Group[3]	Members
6	Prince of Peace 2009 Harvard Corpus Christi, TX 78416	1962	MC	53
6	United Box 883 Premont, TX 78375	1928	MB, MC	50
6	El Mesias Iglesia Menonita 1232 Dakota Robstown, TX 78380	1974	MC	41
6	Calvary 703 W. San Patricia Ave. Mathis, TX 78368	1944	MC	148
7	Carlsbad 2611 Westernway Carlsbad, NM 88220	1967	MC	49
7	Iglesia Evangelica Menonita 204 S. Cypress St. Carlsbad, NM 88220	1979	MC	4
8	Shalom 2902 19th St. Tucson, AZ 95716	1978	GC, MC	18
8	Koinonia Fellowship 1920 E. Colgate Dr. Tempe, AZ 85283	1976	GC, MC	30
8	Sunnyslope 828 E. Brown St. Phoenix, AZ 85020	1946	MC	219

Ch.	Congregation[2]	Begun	Group[3]	Members
8	Trinity 4334 W. Vista Ave. Glendale, AZ 85301	1963	MC	207
8	Iglesia Menonita Emmanuel Box 1695 Surprise, AZ 85345	1972	MC	19
9	Mountain View Box 176 Upland, CA 91786	1934	MC	84
9	Calvary 2400 W. 85th St. Inglewood, CA 90305	1921	MC	128
10	College Community 2529 Willow Ave. Clovis, CA 93612	1963	MB	160
10	Reedley 1362 L. St. Reedley, CA 93654	1905	MB	1,381
11	Haight-Ashbury 450 Scott St. San Francisco, CA 94117	1976	MC	9
12	Albany 3405 Kizer Ave. Albany, OR 97321	1899	MC	197
13	South Seattle 3715 S. 198 St. Seattle, WA 98188	1968	GC	66

Ch.	Congregation[2]	Begun	Group[3]	Members
14	Peace 11571 Daniels Rd Richmond, B.C.	1980	GC	135
15	Mountain View 892 Montford Rd. Kalispell, MT 59901	1913	MC	95
16	Bridgeway Community 510 13 Ave. N.E. Swift Current, Saskatchewan	1934	MB	220
17	Fort Garry Fellowship 117 Lanark St. Winnipeg, Manitoba R3N 1K9	1967	GC	67
18	Steinbach Box 8 Steinbach, Manitoba R0A 2A0	1874	EMCC	550
18	Prairie Rose Landmark Manitoba R0A 0X0	1918	EMCC	330
18	Blumenort Box 114 Blumenort, Manitoba R0A 0C0	1874	EMCC	529

1. Sources of information: *Calendar of Activities*, 1978-79 (Mennonite Brethren); *EMC Yearbook*, 1979 (Evangelical Mennonite Conference); *Handbook of Information*, 1978-1980 (General Conference Mennonite Church); *Mennonite Yearbook*, 1980 (Mennonite Church).

2. Address is either church office, or pastor or other official.

3. General Conference Mennonite Church (GC), Mennonite Church (MC), Mennonite Brethren Church (MB), Evangelical Mennonite Conference of Canada (EMCC).

The Author

Daniel Hertzler has served the Mennonite Church since 1973 as editor of its official weekly magazine, *Gospel Herald*. He has also been acting president of the Mennonite Board of Education, a member of the Goshen College Board of Overseers, and moderator of Allegheny Mennonite Conference

Born on a farm near Elverson, Pennsylvania, in 1925, Hertzler dropped out of high school after the sophomore year and spent the next five years farming. Dan studied at Eastern Mennonite College, Harrisonburg, Virginia, from 1947 to 1952, majoring in Bible. He married Mary Yoder of Streetsboro, Ohio, in July 1952 and began employment the following September at Mennonite Publishing House, Scottdale, Pennsylvania.

His first assignment at Scottdale was as office editor of *Mennonite Community Magazine* (1952-53). He was assistant editor of *Christian Living* from 1954 through 1960, and its editor from 1960 to 1973. He also edited *Children's Uniform Lessons* (1957-59), *Youth Uniform Lessons* (1957-62), *Adult Uniform Lessons* (1957-71), and *Builder* (1964-72).

Hertzler received the BD degree from Goshen College Biblical Seminary following a study leave (1954-55). From 1960 to 1966 he pursued religious education interests at University of Pittsburgh and received the PhD degree. He has also studied at Pittsburgh Theological Seminary (1978-79).

Dan and Mary are members of the Kingview Mennonite Church (he was assistant pastor there, 1952-54). They are the parents of four grown sons: Dennis, Ronald, Gerald, and Dan Mark. Dan's interests include beekeeping, gardening, and nut trees.